FAST TRACK TO SUCCESS

MANAGING PEOPLE & PERFORMANCE

FAST TRACK TO SUCCESS

MANAGING

PEOPLE &

PERFORMANCE

DAVID ROSS

**Financial Times
Prentice Hall
is an imprint of**

Harlow, England • London • New York • Boston • San Francisco • Toronto • Sydney • Singapore • Hong Kong
Tokyo • Seoul • Taipei • New Delhi • Cape Town • Madrid • Mexico City • Amsterdam • Munich • Paris • Milan

PEARSON EDUCATION LIMITED

Edinburgh Gate
Harlow CM20 2JE
Tel: +44 (0)1279 623623
Fax: +44 (0)1279 431059
Website: www.pearsoned.co.uk

First published in Great Britain in 2010

ISBN: 978-0-273-73288-4

British Library Cataloguing-in-Publication Data
A catalogue record for this book is available from the British Library

Library of Congress Cataloging-in-Publication Data
Ross, David.
 Fast track to success : people and performance management / David Ross. -- 1st ed.
      p. cm.
   Includes index.
   ISBN 978-0-273-73288-4 (pbk.)
  1. Employee motivation. 2. Performance technology--Management. 3. Teams in the workplace. 4. Leadership. 5. Organizational effectiveness. I. Title.
   HF5549.5.M63R677 2010
   658.3'14--dc22
                                                          2010026323

10 9 8 7 6 5 4 3 2 1
14 13 12 11 10

Series text design by Design Deluxe
Typeset in 10/15 Swis Lt by 30
Printed by Ashford Colour Press Ltd., Gosport

CONTENTS

THE FAST TRACK WAY

Everything you need to accelerate your career

The best way to fast track your career as a manager is to fast track the contribution you and your team make to your organisation and for your team to be successful in as public a way as possible. That's what the Fast Track series is about. The Fast Track manager delivers against performance expectations, is personally highly effective and efficient, develops the full potential of their team, is recognised as a key opinion leader in the business, and ultimately progresses up the organisation ahead of their peers.

You will benefit from the books in the Fast Track series whether you are an ambitious first-time team leader or a more experienced manager who is keen to develop further over the next few years. You may be a specialist aiming to master every aspect of your chosen discipline or function, or simply be trying to broaden your awareness of other key management disciplines and skills. In either case, you will have the motivation to critically review yourself and your team using the tools and techniques presented in this book, as well as the time to stop, think and act on areas you identify for improvement.

Do you know what you need to know and do to make a real difference to your performance at work, your contribution to your company and your blossoming career? For most of us, the honest answer is 'Not really, no'. It's not surprising then that most of us never reach our full potential. The innovative Fast Track series gives you exactly what you need to speed up your progress and become a high performance manager in all the areas of the business that matter. Fast Track is not just another 'How to' series. Books on selling tell you how to win sales but not how to move from salesperson to sales manager. Project management software enables you to plan detailed tasks but doesn't improve the quality of your project management thinking and business performance. A marketing book tells you about the principles of marketing but not how to lead a team of marketers. It's not enough.

Specially designed features in the Fast Track books will help you to see what you need to know and to develop the skills you need to be successful. They give you:

→ the information required for you to shine in your chosen function or skill – particularly in the Fast Track top ten;

→ practical advice in the form of Quick Tips and answers to FAQs from people who have been there before you and succeeded;

→ state of the art best practice as explained by today's academics and industry experts in specially written Expert Voices;

→ case stories and examples of what works and, perhaps more importantly, what doesn't work;

→ comprehensive tools for accelerating the effectiveness and performance of your team;

→ a framework that helps you to develop your career as well as produce terrific results.

Fast Track is a resource of business thinking, approaches and techniques presented in a variety of ways – in short, a complete performance support environment. It enables managers to build careers from their first tentative steps into management all the way up to becoming a business director – accelerating the performance of their team and their career. When you use the Fast Track approach with your team it provides a common business language and structure, based on best business practice. You will benefit from the book whether or not others in the organisation adopt the same practices; indeed if they don't, it will give you an edge over them. Each Fast Track book blends hard practical advice from expert practitioners with insights and the latest thinking from experts from leading business schools.

The Fast Track approach will be valuable to team leaders and managers from all industry sectors and functional areas. It is for ambitious people who have already acquired some team leadership skills and have realised just how much more there is to know.

If you want to progress further you will be directed towards additional learning and development resources via an interactive Fast Track website, **www.Fast-Track-Me.com**. For many, these books therefore become the first step in a journey of continuous development. So, the Fast Track approach gives you everything you need to accelerate your career, offering you the opportunity to develop your knowledge and skills, improve your team's performance, benefit your organisation's progress towards its aims and light the fuse under your true career potential.

ABOUT THE AUTHOR

DAVID ROSS established Performance Unlimited in 1993 as a coaching organisation centred on his unique coaching model that pioneers corporate leadership coaching and delivers coaching development solutions to executive leadership communities in banking, pharmaceuticals, food and beverage, IT and Telcos, as well as some public sector organisations.

The company's unique proposition is to enable individuals to develop behaviour change that complements their strengths and is totally aligned to the business results that they and their organisations want them to achieve.

This trademarked model, 'Six Steps to Unlimited Performance'®, forms the lynchpin of the company's success in helping businesses and the individuals that run them to achieve their objectives and improve their performance. Having created such a powerful and effective tool, it is not surprising that David has great enthusiasm for and commitment to executive coaching and is much in demand on the lecture circuit.

'Our unique proposition is to enable individuals to develop behaviour change that complements their strengths and is totally aligned to the business results that they and their organisations want them to achieve.'

High Performance Leadership is a five-step transformational programme which delivers lasting results throughout the organisation.

Traditional leadership team development programmes take too long to deliver. Because High Performance Leadership is a truly integrated approach to developing high-performing teams and organisations, it accelerates the time it takes to build a high-performing team and will have a measurable impact in your current financial year.

A planned, progressive programme of leadership development and shared culture, High Performance Leadership includes all the team and individual interventions required to bring about sustainable improvements in performance and ensure you get rapid results for your business.

High Performance Leadership is underpinned by distinctive, web-based software which helps you sustain improvements in your core processes.

A WORD OF THANKS FROM THE AUTHOR

I would like to thank the following for their generous contributions to this book.

→ **Liz Gooster, Pearson.** There are many exciting new ideas in the publishing world at present, but without an enthusiastic champion, most will simply die a slow death. Liz had the confidence to commission the Fast Track series and associated web-tool on behalf of the Pearson Group at a time when other publishers were cutting back on non-core activities. She has remained committed to its success – providing direction, challenge and encouragement as and when required.

→ **Ken Langdon.** As well as being a leading author in his own right, Ken has worked with all the Fast Track authors to bring a degree of rigour and consistency to the series. As each book has developed, he has been a driving force behind the scenes, pulling the detailed content for each title together in the background – working with an equal measure of enthusiasm and patience!

→ **Mollie Dickenson.** Mollie has a background in publishing and works as a research manager at Henley Business School, and has been a supporter of the project from its inception. She has provided constant encouragement and challenge, and is, as always, an absolute delight to work with.

→ **Critical readers.** As the Fast Track series evolved, it was vital that we received constant challenge and input from other experts and from critical readers.

→ **Professor David Birchall.** David has worked to identify and source Expert Voice contributions from international academic and business experts in each Fast Track title. David is co-author of the Fast Track *Innovation* book and a leading academic author in his own right, and has spent much of the last 20 years heading up the research programme at Henley Business School – one of the world's top ten business schools.

Our expert team

Last but not least, I am grateful for the contributions made by experts from around the world in each of the Fast Track titles.

EXPERT	TOPIC	BUSINESS SCHOOL/ COMPANY
Dr Liz Houldsworth	A commentary on measuring performance – the trend towards forced distribution (p. 14)	Henley Business School, University of Reading
Dr Lynn Thurloway and Dr Jean-Anne Stewart	Generation Y and Z: Who are they? Should we manage them differently? (p. 24)	Henley Business School, University of Reading
Dr Richard McBain	Engagement, commitment and the line manager (p. 69)	Henley Business School, University of Reading
Nick Horslen	Managing future performance through an emergent workforce (p. 86)	Independent business adviser
Professor Roger Palmer	Managing marketing performance (p. 104)	Henley Business School, University of Reading
Dr Serge Besanger	Managing people the Socratic way (p. 127)	ESSEC Asia-Pacific
Professor Mike Pedler	Creating a learning organisation (p. 148)	Henley Business School, University of Reading
Professor Victor Dulewicz	The competencies method for assessing staff (p. 165)	Henley Business School, University of Reading

MANAGING PEOPLE & PERFORMANCE FAST TRACK

Just why do some teams produce excellent results and some just mediocre or poor results? Why are there some star divisions in a company and some millstones? Why, in the end, do some organisations operate so much more effectively and efficiently than others? The answer is so simple that everyone fundamentally knows it. Because people are different and getting the best possible performance from them is a great skill. You can help most people to achieve excellence, even those who, to begin with, are coasting or behaving in a way that is actually counterproductive to the business.

To be competitive nowadays you need more top players than poor players in the team. In this book I will describe team members as A, B and C players, explain the rationale behind this and its usefulness. But the main thrust of the book is to explain the processes to use in order to produce the best performance possible out of most of the people in your team. It's quite individualised since not only do you need to implement the processes with everyone but you also have to know how to get each individual team member to use them well and achieve excellence. They will all do that slightly differently. We start from getting everyone to understand their role and responsibility within the team with a complete understanding of their focus and the measures by which their performance will be measured. Then going through a series of steps we arrive at what I call a unique social system where each team member knows the others very well and there is a high level of trust.

There are six behavioural dimensions that characterise a high performing team.

Dimension 1: An overriding sense of purpose

By sharing an understanding of individual workloads and visions, the team also shares a commitment to that vision and the team's goals. Members will also know how each of them is motivated to achieve the desired results. Clarity is the watchword here: clarity of business purpose, strategic priorities, the required standards of performance and, finally, clarity of the measurable results members are going to deliver.

Dimension 2: Building on strengths and skills

There is one team leader with overall responsibility for decision making and appointing new team members to the team. The leader coaches team members. Each team member takes leadership in some aspect of teamwork where they have a special technical skill or a particular talent. The team understands the technical competencies of each of its members and how and when to utilise those competencies in the pursuit of the common goals.

The team leader is in the end accountable for how the team runs and performs, making sure that the resources are there to make achievement of its shared goals as certain as is possible in a business world of risk. This leads to the development of further competencies.

Dimension 3: A strong results ethic

Each member of the team has a clear set of objectives that contributes to the overall goals for the team. It is crucial for these to be written down and agreed by each individual and used in a systematic approach to measuring performance. Go back to the processes, ensuring that those processes critical to establishing a common pattern and way of achieving certain goals are well understood and are simple to follow.

A passion for success leads people to work beyond these agreed objectives by putting in extra, or discretionary, effort for no set reward because they are committed and love what they are doing. New team members are well received and go through a process to get them up to the requirements and values of the team. This focus on results does not prevent team members displaying empathy for other team members – offering them support, for example, when they are emotionally or personally challenged.

As work proceeds and the team is closing in on delivering the results, they continuously look for ways of improving the processes and tasks or even the climate the team is working in to achieve success. When success comes they celebrate their achievements both individually and collectively.

As they move on, teams approach problems with a creative mindset, looking for solutions that take the business forward, beyond where it is now.

Dimension 4: Open communication and mutual accountability

In a high-performing team, personal agendas stay out of the room and team members operate on the basis of common goals. They share their skills. People recognise the individual skills or specialist knowledge that other team members bring and want to utilise those effectively to get the best results. People talk about their feelings and are open about them whether positive or negative.

Members focus on the issue and don't waste time going 'off piste' in an environment that enables them to give feedback on team issues.

Dimension 5: A cohesive, compassionate and unified team

The team leader is the ultimate authority when making final decisions or hiring new team members: beyond that there are no obvious hierarchies. The team is naturally motivated to become high performing and does whatever is necessary to improve performance.

The team shares and takes considered risks. The team knows how to generate options to arrive at the optimal path to achieve its goals. It evaluates those options sufficiently well to mitigate the risks associated with those options that are untried and new ways of getting to the goals.

Dimension 6: Unique social system

The team actively encourages and benefits from diversity by selecting team members of diverse culture, race, personality, talent and skills in order to have the best chance of success. Members believe that they know, trust and respect each other. Team members have taken the time to get to know each other at the level of personality, values, experience, knowledge, talent and skills. They have developed an acceptance of their differences.

Members enjoy working and playing together. They enjoy working on goals and projects together as well as the social moments that they can share together. They agree that those moments are part of the social structure of the team.

First class performance management needs champions, people who will drive through the problems and setbacks, convince sceptics of the need to do new things and make a good idea produce results. Perhaps you are that champion: perhaps just for your team or division of your company, or perhaps for the entire organisation. If so, you have an exciting time ahead. Remember, once a great idea is recorded it can never die; but there's a lot to get right before you can be sure that it will fly: so let's get on with it.

HOW TO USE THIS BOOK

Fast Track books present a collection of the latest tools, techniques and advice to help build your team and your career. Use this table to plan your route through the book.

PART	OVERVIEW
About the authors	A brief overview of the authors, their background and their contact details
A **Awareness**	*This first part gives you an opportunity to gain a quick overview of the topic and to reflect on your current effectiveness*
1 *Performance management in a nutshell*	A brief overview of performance management and a series of frequently asked questions to bring you up to speed quickly
2 *Performance management audit*	Simple checklists to help identify strengths and weaknesses in your team and your capabilities
B **Business Fast Track**	*Part B provides tools and techniques that may form part of the integrated performance management framework for you and your team*
3 *Fast Track top ten*	Ten tools and techniques used to help you implement a sustainable approach to performance management based on the latest best practice
4 *Technologies*	A review of the latest information technologies used to improve effectiveness and efficiency of performance management activities
5 *Implementing change*	A detailed checklist to identify gaps and to plan the changes necessary to implement your projects
C **Career Fast Track**	*Part C focuses on you, your leadership qualities and what it takes to get to the top*
6 *The first ten weeks*	Recommended activities when starting a new role in performance management, together with a checklist of useful facts to know
7 *Leading the team*	Managing change, building your team and deciding your leadership style
8 *Getting to the top*	Becoming a performance management professional, getting promoted and becoming a director – what does it take?
D **Director's toolkit**	*The final part provides more advanced tools and techniques based on industry best practice*
Toolkit	Advanced tools and techniques used by senior managers
Glossary	Glossary of terms

FAST-TRACK-ME.COM

Before reading this book, why not start by visiting our companion website **www.Fast-Track-Me.com**? This is a custom-designed, highly interactive online resource that addresses the needs of the busy manager by providing access to ideas and methods that will

improve individual and team performance quickly, and develop both your skills and your career.

As well as giving you access to cutting-edge business knowledge across a range of key topics – including the subject of this book – **Fast-Track-Me.com** will enable you to stop and think about what you want to achieve in your chosen career and where you want to take your team. By doing this, it will provide a context for reading and give you extra information and access to a range of interactive features.

The site in general is packed with valuable features, such as:

→ **The Knowledge Cube**. The K-Cube is a two-dimensional matrix presenting Fast Track features from all topics in a consistent and easy-to-use way – providing ideas, tools and techniques in a single place, anytime, anywhere. This is a great way to delve in and out of business topics quickly.

→ **The Online Coach**. The Online Coach is a toolkit of fully inter-active business templates in MS Word format that allow Fast-Track-Me.com users to explore specific business methods (strategy, ideas, projects etc.) and learn from concepts, case examples and other resources according to your preferred learning style.

→ **Business Glossary**. The Fast Track Business Glossary pro-vides a comprehensive list of key words associated with each title in the Fast Track series together with a plain English defini-tion – helping you to cut through business jargon.

To access even more features, carry out self-diagnostic tests and develop your own personal profile, simply log-in and register – then click on My FastTrack to get started! Give yourself the Fast Track Health Check now.

My FastTrack

These are the different areas you'll discover in the My FastTrack area.

My HealthCheck

How effective is your team compared with industry 'best practices'? Find out using a simple Red, Amber, Green (RAG) scale.

After identifying areas of concern, you can plan for their resolution using a personal 'Get2Green' action plan.

My Get2Green Actions

What are the specific actions you and your team will implement in order to 'Get2Green' and improve performance? Log, prioritise and monitor your action points in the My Get2Green Action Plan area to help you plan for future success – fast.

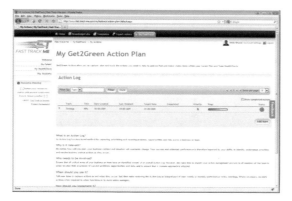

My Career

Reflect on your current role and plan your future career – how prepared are you for future success?

Fast-Track-Me.com provides the busy manager with access to the latest thinking, techniques and tools at their fingertips. It can also help answer some of the vital questions managers are asking themselves today.

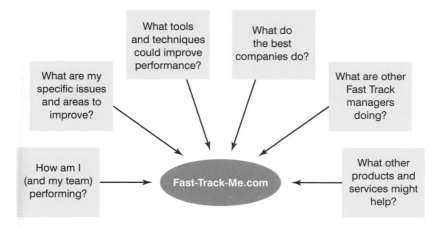

Don't get left behind: log on to **www.Fast-Track-Me.com** now to get your career on the fast track.

PART A

AWARENESS

This book introduces a sustainable approach to performance management aimed at keeping you, your team and your organisation at the forefront of getting the best people performance possible, thus contributing towards the future of all three. The starting point is to gain a quick understanding of what performance management is and what it is not, and to be aware of your own and your team's capabilities in this area right now. For this reason I will ask you a number of questions that will reveal where you and your team need to improve if you are to truly have a culture of top-flight performance management and meet the aims of your organisation – exciting product sets for your customers and business processes in place that put your people and your service to customers amongst the leaders in your industry.

'Know yourself' was the motto above the doorway of the Oracle at Delphi and is a wise thought. It means that you must do an open and honest self-audit as you start on the process of setting up your framework for performance management.

The stakes are high. People performance is at the heart of success in this global, competitive marketplace. Your team, therefore, need to be effective performers and you need to be a good leader. Poor leadership and poor team effectiveness will make failure likely. An effective team poorly led will sap the team's energy and lead in the long term to failure through members leaving for a better environment or becoming less effective through lack of motivation. Leading an ineffective team well does not prevent the obvious conclusion that an ineffective team will not thrive. So, looking at the figure below, how do you make sure that you and your team are in the top right-hand box – a top performing and effective team with an excellent leader? That's what this book is about and this part shows you how to discover your and your team's starting point.

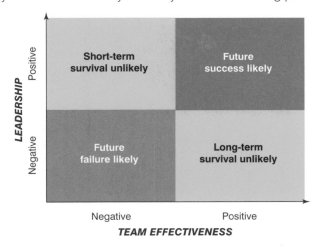

1

PERFORMANCE MANAGEMENT IN A NUTSHELL

Performance management is an essential component of building successful teams and getting consistently great results. If you don't set the benchmark for great performance then people will default to their own standards that may well be very different to your own expectations of the behaviours and actions that deliver great results. Remember that everyone has their own unique model of the world.

Starting with the basics

A three-fold win

The benefits of managing performance well give a three-fold win: the individual makes the most of their skills and improves their career potential; the team improves its performance and produces a higher performance than the sum of its parts; and the organisation simply gets better results.

Performance can only be measured through an equation that makes it explicit:

→ What is the specific outcome you want to achieve or that you want the person concerned to achieve? The outcome will have a set of criteria that you agree with the person relating to what you will see, feel and hear that lets you know the outcome was achieved.

→ What is the style in which you want them to achieve it? For example, is it important to build, sustain and maintain relationships with those around you as you move towards the outcome? You may want to establish behavioural ground rules as part of the way in which you measure their performance.

Managing performance can only happen effectively if you know what excellent performance looks like and you have agreed the criteria with the person concerned. As you will see in Chapter 3, individual performance can only be mapped effectively if the bigger picture framework of the team or company's future direction has been set.

Managing performance requires other activities that you need to commit to if you are going to do it well:

→ Build an effective relationship with the individuals whose performance you are going to manage. They need to be able to relate to you, trust you and you need to be able to communicate with them in a way that speaks to their model of the world.

→ Be prepared to give feedback on their performance regularly. Don't wait until performance reviews to give people feedback. They won't thank you for telling them what they need to know six months or a year down the line. 'The reason you are getting a 2% increase in salary instead of 6% is because you failed to meet deadlines set for the key tasks you were given and you have failed consistently all year.'

→ Monitor performance regularly, at least monthly, so that you are able to measure the overall performance of the team through each individual's monthly tasks or other forms of targets. Keep a record of this performance and your conversations around performance.

→ Hold quarterly performance reviews with the team and the individuals.

A, B and C players

A word about A, B and C players. We use the terms to describe a person in terms of their competencies, their attitude and their talents and strengths. There is more on this in Chapter 3. At this stage here is a summary of the competency part of the analysis:

→ An 'A' player is someone who exceeds expectations in 50 per cent or more of the skills required to perform the role.

→ A 'B' player is one who is good to very good in 50 per cent or more of the skills required to perform the role.

→ A 'C' player is below the level of a 'B' player and is someone who is good/average in 50 per cent or more of the skills. The role of a 'C' player is to support a 'B' player. You would not have 'C' players in leadership roles in your high-performing team. If they can play a useful support role, then it may well be right to keep them in a high-performing team. If they cannot do that, move them on to a more suitable role.

 CASE STORY **TAKE RADICAL ACTION IF IT'S NEEDED, LOUISE'S STORY**

Narrator Louise took over a successful team selling complex hardware and software to government agencies.

Context On the face of it everything looked rather good. The team had good results and had a salesperson, Jan, who was one of the leading salespeople in the country.

Issue Jan plainly had a very influential role in the team. Everyone in the team approached him for advice. In fact people seemed incapable of deciding a sales strategy or any major decision without consulting Jan. Using a process to identify the A, B and C players in the team, Louise found that there were several B players who were potential A players but were held back by their deference to Jan. Jan was an A player by results but not by any measure of 'being a good team member.' Louise was concerned at the dominance of one person who seemed to be holding other members of the team back.

Solution To the surprise of everyone Louise moved Jan out of the team. She allocated the accounts that he serviced to other salespeople and brought in a new salesperson who was showing a lot of potential. The effect was like a dam breaking. New ideas flowed from people who had been, in effect, bottled up by Jan. More A players emerged and the team's results went from strength to strength.

Learning An analytical approach to the categorisation of people can reveal an action plan that appears on the face of it counter-intuitive. At the same time as learning this, remember the trauma and difficulty of managing the process of removing someone from a team.

Major trends

Over the past decade, there have been three major trends that mean that it is increasingly important to define, manage and track the performance of your team and your people:

1 All industry sectors are becoming more and more competitive. Poor performance will result in a gradual decline in sales, a movement towards increasingly small niche markets and, ultimately, financial failure and business collapse. There are no hiding places. This has resulted in a relentless drive towards improving effectiveness and efficiency across all business teams, where processes, systems and skills are being redefined. Creative and process thinking are becoming more critical to success where project management, risk management and innovation are becoming core team skills – enabling companies to deliver what they say they are going to deliver, on time and within budget. Most organisations are also experimenting with and applying more sophisticated techniques, but these tend to come and go with business fashion and do not interfere with the basics of achieving high-performing teams.

2 Companies face increasing expectations from their customers and consumers: they have got used to continuous improvement in what the business world offers them. They are better informed about possibilities because of access to information – in part fuelled by the internet which offers opportunities for product/

price comparisons that were impossible in the days when the only way you could get such information was from biased advertisements and walking round the shops. Put simply, consumers want more for less, and consumers want it faster. They won't accept mediocrity because if we can't deliver, someone else will. Not only does this affect the skills your team will require, it changes how they need to behave and the attitudes they need to bring to work each day.

3 Finally comes globalisation: no matter how big or small you are, you are now competing in a global market. The corner shop, struggling with having to charge higher prices because it lacks the buying muscle of the big boys, is now also competing head-to-head with sellers on eBay and with national retailers offering home delivery. The labour market is also international, and your team may comprise talented people from all over the world – each bringing different skills and approaches to working.

Gary Hamel summed up the challenge that businesses face as: 'Those that live by the sword will be shot by those that don't!'[1] My conclusion is that if you can't compete on the basis of price, you have to offer an excellent and differentiated product and service, and to do this you need highly motivated people working within high-performing teams.

> QUICK TIP **BUSINESS ENVIRONMENT**
> Constant monitoring of your business environment will help to identify significant ideas for change (opportunities and threats). Look for trends and ask: 'So what? How will this impact me or my team?'

What typically goes wrong?

So, recognising how important people and performance management is to the future success of a company and your team, let's take a panoramic view by looking first at what can go wrong. This should make you think about particular areas in your business or team where one or more of these problems occur and focus your attention on fixing them. Then

[1] Hamel, G. (2002) *Leading the Revolution*, Boston, MA: Harvard Business School Press.

we'll look at a number of frequently asked questions to finish off this rapid introduction to the topic.

1 **The overall business or team strategy is unclear.** Many successful teams grow on the basis of yesterday's performance. Whilst historic success is to be applauded, it does not guarantee future success. Teams need to have clarity of vision and purpose, and need to constantly adapt to changes in their environment.

2 **There are no agreed performance targets.** Even when there is a team strategy in place, unless this is translated into clear targets that are understood and agreed by the team, individual members are likely to work in ways that maximise their individual performance but at the expense of the team's overall performance.

3 **Teams are not structured for optimum performance.** The way that roles and responsibilities are defined and the group is structured often reflects historical needs. Just as the strategy needs to change to reflect the current business requirements, the team structure should be continually reviewed.

4 **Those with the greatest talent are underutilised.** Whilst each member of the team will contribute to the overall success of the team, they are all different and will each contribute varying amounts. To optimise performance, it is vital to get the right people into the right roles, and to develop them to the maximum of their ability.

5 **People are resistant to change.** Resistance to change reflects an attitude that slows or stops the development of a team. As customer expectations change, and competitor performance improves, businesses must adapt. Not doing so will result in long-term or short-term failure.

6 **There is no structured development programme.** There is a common phrase that 'practice makes perfect'. Unfortunately this is not true. As your team gains experience through repeated completion of tasks, its performance will initially improve, but then will quickly plateau. It is only through training in 'best practice, coaching and feedback' that team performance will approach 'perfect'.

7 **Performance is not reviewed on a regular basis.** Setting clear targets alone will not guarantee that they will be achieved. High-performance teams will monitor performance on a regular basis, and will use the reviews to identify areas of concern actions necessary to improve performance.

8 **There is no effective process of governance.** Most teams are poor at conducting their regular (monthly) performance review meetings. The wrong people turn up, the wrong items are on the agenda, and the meeting runs badly.

So just what is performance management? – frequently asked questions

The following table provides quick answers to some of the most frequently asked questions about the topic of people and performance management. Use this as a way of gaining a quick overview.

FAQ 1 What do we mean by performance management?	1 Performance management can best be described as a professional and systematic way of getting people to perform to their best and achieve the highest success possible. It includes building high-performing teams through using processes and concentrating on the behaviours necessary to be high achievers.
FAQ 2 Why is performance management important to our business, when profits and revenues are good?	2 The pace of change in business today is phenomenal. What is profitable and successful today may be out of date or copied by competitors tomorrow. Performance management is the key to differentiation, and differentiation is the key to staying ahead.
FAQ 3 Who should be involved in performance management?	3 Everyone! If you can create a culture of high-performing teams where it is part of the DNA of your business, then you stand a better chance of becoming more and more successful. You may start with a few 'performance advocates' around the business, but the best achieving companies are widely conscious of good performance management.
FAQ 4 How do I confirm individual key performance objectives and key performance indicators?	4 Develop a written plan for the year that confirms what the key performance objectives are, stating clearly what it is you want the team to achieve. Make sure that you detail the key performance indicators for each objective. This gives the evidence for success of each objective.

FAQ 5 What's the difference between talent and competence?	5 The difference is that a competence is a learned skill that is developed through experience. A person can be poor, average, good or excellent at a competence. There is a range of competencies required for any role. A talent is an innate, naturally occurring set of competencies learned during the formative period of a person's life, usually between birth and 14 years old. It's something that a person is naturally excellent at doing.
FAQ 6 If I am taking over a team from someone else, how do I start?	6 First, review the overall framework of objectives and strategies and the performance of individuals in the team. Make sure that you leave people in no doubt that you are taking responsibility and in so doing will take responsibility adopting your own framework not someone else's.
FAQ 7 Can I create my own strategic framework in isolation from the rest of the business?	7 No, make sure that you understand the overall vision for the business and what the strategic priorities are for the business as a whole. If there is no framework, then influence people to conceive of one. In the worst case develop one for yourself and let others notice the difference between your results and theirs.
FAQ 8 Should I make the concept of 'A', 'B' and 'C' players overt to the team?	8 No you should not, unless this is an HR policy supported by the overall business. Use the concept informally rather than formally.
FAQ 9 What if there is no succession planning process in the overall business?	9 Carry on and create your own, otherwise you won't have the means to move on yourself. Get yourself the reputation of being a net exporter of talent from your team. That way people will want to join knowing that you will look after their careers.
FAQ 10 Why should I give positive feedback regularly even when little has been achieved or little progress made?	10 When used appropriately, positive feedback reinforces good behaviour and generates a lot of motivation energy. You make people aware when they are behaving in the way you and the rest of the team want. Do this regularly and people will put it into a better context when you have to talk about underperformance.
FAQ 11 What do I do if an individual consistently underperforms?	11 Make sure that you have given clear feedback and are clear with them about the consequences of not improving. Commit to coaching them for a period of three months. If after three months of coaching and support the person's performance does not improve, either move them into a more suitable role or move them out of the business.

FAQ 12 *Can I include measures of quality as well as hard numeric indicators in a person's objectives?*	12 Certainly you can. Try to find some concrete measures as well, but in the end an objective on, for example, customer satisfaction is sometimes best measured by talking to the customers themselves. Quality can be measured by comparison with the competition, but again there's bound to be a woolly element to that.
FAQ 13 *Why do some teams achieve a really good 'team spirit' while others don't?*	13 In some ways this is the $64,000 question. As well as putting in first-class processes that encourage excellent performance, involve all team members in the running of the team and slowly introduce a culture where everyone takes a pride in their work. This book is pretty much an amplification of this principle.
FAQ 14 *Do social activities have a place in modern team management, given the curbs on expenses?*	14 Yes, you have got to find the money for such crucial events in some way or other. Look for other budget savings and tell people what you are going to spend the saved money on.
FAQ 15 *Is it easier to take over a well-functioning team rather than one that has problems?*	15 Probably it is easier to take over the problematic team because you can find out what the problem is and fix it. Taking over a well-functioning team means understanding what makes it tick, keeping that going and adding your own fresh ideas into the mix.
FAQ 16 *Who should I help first – the poor performers, the average performers or the best people?*	16 First look for ways to improve the performance of the average team members. After all, that will have the biggest affect on your results. Helping poor performers is time-consuming and if they cannot change, then you have wasted that time trying to get the benefit of making a poor performer into an average one.
FAQ 17 *What are the main attributes of a good team leader?*	17 Funnily enough, at the most basic level the main attribute is listening. Listen to other team members, your customers and your suppliers and you will start to identify the right strategy. It then becomes your job to drive that strategy through.
FAQ 18 *Is it best to offer bonuses for team performance or individual performance?*	18 Both can be useful, but trying to get team bonuses right so that no one feels that they should have been paid more and another person paid less is difficult – it is not a trivial pursuit.
FAQ 19 *Should I publish each team member's performance publicly?*	19 Look very carefully at the context and skills of your team before you do this. I've seen it work in a sales environment but fail horribly in others.
FAQ 20 *Is it possible to get a team to discuss each other's strengths and weaknesses without falling out?*	20 It certainly is, but you really need to read the book to understand thoroughly how to do it.

I hope these FAQs give a quick start to getting to grips with people and performance management. The rest of this book shows you how to move from understanding what the key elements are to an active implementation of good performance management either within your team, division- or company-wide if that is your role.

QUICK TIP BUSINESS ENVIRONMENT
First-class team management is a long and very satisfying challenge. Take it step by step.

A commentary on measuring performance – the trend towards forced distribution

Dr Liz Houldsworth Henley Business School, University of Reading

We all know the old story of call-centre operators allegedly pushing customers quickly off the phone in order to meet their targets for 'pick up time' and 'throughput of calls'. Such behaviour has been described as 'measurement dysfunction', whereby effort is put into 'managing the measure' rather than 'managing performance'. It might be expected that the trend towards more 'objective' and measurement-based approaches to performance management will see off this sort of behaviour. In our research with organisations,[2] we report on how the trend towards globalisation has led increasingly to attempts to standardise performance management approaches and ensure consistency. This drive for standardisation is consistent with more measurement-based approaches, typically underpinned by role specifications and competency definitions applied in different international locations.

Of course the drive for standardisation applies to the objective-setting phase (planning) of performance management, but even more so to the

[2] Houldsworth, E. and Jirasinghe, D. (2006) *Managing and Measuring Employee Performance: Lessons from Research into HR Practice*, London: Kogan Page.

review and reward component of the cycle. Anecdotally we are told that the majority of line managers would prefer a trip to the dentist than to have to conduct a performance review: this is likely to be even more the case where there are performance issues to be discussed.

It is not uncommon for managers to avoid such performance discussions and, as a result, all employees become rated as 'good' or 'above average' – thus resulting in what commentators describe as 'ratings drift'.

A common way of tackling rating drift and injecting a bit more realism into performance distributions is to provide guidance on the range of distributions expected. At its most stringent, this may resemble the 'vitality curve' (also known as 'rank and yank') approach adopted by General Electric (GE) under the leadership of Jack Welch in the 1990s.[3] Under this approach, managers at GE were directed to rank all their direct reports in terms of the top 20 per cent, the core 70 per cent and the bottom 10 per cent. The bottom 10 per cent was then expected to be removed from the organisation.

There is a considerable debate about forced distribution. Some US firms have now stopped using forced ranking altogether, but on this side of the Atlantic things appear to be moving in the opposite direction.

Forced ranking may take a variety of forms. While some organisations use a GE-style 20-70-10 system – with or without the associated 'yanking' – others allocate staff to a larger number of categories. Then there are those who use a purer form of ranking, so that if there are, say, 50 people in a work group, they will all be ranked from 1 to 50. Central to all these systems is the idea of judging employees not only against absolute standards but also on how they compare with their peers. Both approaches require careful implementation and training for line managers. In addition, it is the movement towards forced distribution that has led to the popularisation of 'calibration' or 'moderation' meetings, typically facilitated by HR in order to support consistency across the business.

Whatever your organisation decides, implementation is unlikely to be popular, nor is it likely to be straightforward. Does it provide business benefit? In their book *Hard Facts, Dangerous Half-Truths and Total Nonsense*,[4] Jeffrey Pfeffer and Robert Sutton suggest that there is no proof that forced distribution provides any business benefit. However advocates of the approach claim that forced ranking not only gives employers improved budgetary control, but also enables organisations to identify, reward and retain their most talented people – a key goal for most HR departments today.

[3] Welch, J. and Byrne, J. (2003) *Jack: Straight from the Gut*, New York: Warner Books.
[4] Pfeffer, J. and Sutton, R.L. (2006) *Hard Facts, Dangerous Half Truths and Total Nonsense*, Boston, MA: Harvard Business School Press.

PERFORMANCE MANAGEMENT AUDIT

The purpose of this section is to provide you with some tools and questions to enable you to look for and find the gaps in your team's performance.

The high-performing team questionnaire is designed to enable you to undertake gap analysis and to identify where you are on the journey towards a high-performing environment. You can run this questionnaire with your team and make members part of creating a high-performing team from the beginning. Split your team into two, encourage ideas and then sift them to agree on the action plan you can put into place immediately.

Team assessment

Is my team maximising its potential?

Use the following checklist to assess the current state of your team, considering each element in turn. Use a simple Red-Amber-Green evaluation, where Red reflects areas where you disagree strongly with the statement and there are significant issues requiring immediate attention, Amber suggests areas of concern and risk, and Green means that you are happy with your current state.

QUICK TIP *MAKING A PLAN*
When you are planning a long journey make sure you are completely sure of your starting point.

ID	CATEGORY	EVALUATION CRITERIA	STATUS
PM1	Vision	The team shares the commitment to a clear vision and a clear business purpose. It has defined a strategic framework around which it can build its goals	
PM2	Business DNA	Individuals have key performance indicators (KPIs) that clearly set out what their role in realising the strategy is. The team has a balanced scorecard recording its values not only in financial terms but also in soft-quality measures such as quality, customer satisfaction and job satisfaction	
PM3	High-performance teams	The team has an appropriate structure with agreed plans for the way ahead. It has balance and diversity and each person knows whose particular expertise makes them the leader in certain areas and activities	
PM4	'A' players	I have identified the key contributors. I am developing their leadership skills and thinking about how to manage talent to get the most out of my best people	
PM5	Business continuity	There is a process in place that identifies potential successors in key roles and allows them to develop their leadership roles in that area. We have mitigated the risk of anyone unexpectedly leaving the team	
PM6	Motivating change	Everyone is involved in continuous innovation and the search for ways to improve performance. They are motivated to welcome change and take their part in its implementation	
PM7	Developing people	Everyone has a personal profile and a personal development plan (PDP) that builds on their talents to enhance their knowledge and skills	
PM8	Right behaviours/ right attitudes	We are contributing to necessary changes in the organisation's culture to influence the way people think and act	
PM9	Effective governance	We are compliant with all statutory rules and regulations. We strive to meet with best practice standards and hold regular performance review meetings (PRMs)	
PM10	Gaining visibility	We have access to all the summary information we need and a process to instantly warn us of variations from plan	

Self-assessment

Do I have what it takes?

This section presents a self-assessment checklist against the factors that make a successful Fast Track leader. These reflect the knowledge, competencies, attitudes and behaviours required to get to the top, irrespective of your current level of seniority. Take control of your career, behave professionally, and reflect on your personal vision for the next five years. This creates a framework for action throughout the rest of the book.

Use the following checklist to identify where you personally need to gain knowledge or skills. Fill it in honestly and then get someone who knows you well, your boss or a key member of your team, to go over it with you. Be willing to change your assessment if people give you insights into yourself that you had not taken into account.

Use the following scoring process:

0 Not yet recognised as a required area of knowledge or skill

1 You are aware of the area but have low knowledge and lack skills

2 An area where you are reasonably competent and working on improvement

3 An area where you have a satisfactory level of knowledge and skills

4 You are consistently well above average

5 You are recognised as a key figure in this area of knowledge and skills throughout the business.

Then reflect on the lowest scores and identify those areas that are critical to success. Flag these as status 'Red' requiring immediate attention. Then identify those areas that you are concerned about and flag those as status 'Amber', implying areas of development that need to be monitored closely.

ID	CATEGORY	EVALUATION CRITERIA	SCORE	STATUS
Knowledge			0–5	RAG
K1	Industry and markets	Knowledge of your industry sector in terms of scope (boundaries), overall size and growth, and major trends. This should include an understanding of natural segmentation of products and markets		
K2	Customers and competitors	Information about major customers, in terms of who they are, and their must-haves and wants. Also an understanding of who the best competitors are and what they do. You also know about and supply chain options and capabilities		
K3	Products and services	An understanding of current products and services, and how they perform in the marketplace against the industry leaders. This should include substitutes or solutions available from companies in different industries		
K4	Business drivers	Insights into current and emerging technologies, legislation, environmental and economic trends that will impact on future product design, access to market or process improvements		
Competencies				
C1	Creative thinking	Ability to use various techniques to challenge the current state of your activities, and identify new ways to improve people and performance		
C2	Root cause analysis	Ability to appraise a situation and analyse factors that could enable or cause a dramatic improvement in performance		
C3	Project management	Ability to define, plan, monitor and control change activities in order to deliver identified performance improvements on time and within budget		
C4	Risk management	Ability to think ahead and identify, prioritise and mitigate barriers to effective and enduring implementations of ideas		

ID	CATEGORY	EVALUATION CRITERIA	SCORE	STATUS
Attitudes			0–5	RAG
A1	Positive approach	Belief that you can make a difference and get things done. You avoid looking like a victim of circumstances when you have to overcome resistance from other people	☐	☐
A2	Seeking synergies	Willingness to look for ways to creatively combine several ideas (even if they are other people's) in order to develop a new and exciting concept	☐	☐
A3	Inquisitive mindset	Awareness of the need to constantly seek more effective or efficient ways of doing things. Willingness to challenge the status quo and ask why things are as they are	☐	☐
A4	Breakthrough thinking	Not accepting average or second best. Constantly seeking ways to dramatically change the way things are	☐	☐
Behaviours				
B1	Determination and commitment	Being prepared to see things through. No project goes according to plan; you are not put off by early setbacks or problems – you need resilience	☐	☐
B2	Visible and active support	Making it clear that you are supportive of priority ideas in the way you allocate your time, resources and budgets	☐	☐
B3	Encouraging others	Enthusiastic in coaching and mentoring others who have ideas, or who are involved in the implementation of ideas for performance improvement. Looking for ways in which you can be the catalyst for the team	☐	☐
B4	Positive challenge	Challenging the ideas of others in a positive way, helping them to think differently about the way things are	☐	☐

 CASE STORY **KNOWING THE MINDSET OF YOUR PEOPLE, ELIZABETH'S STORY**

Narrator Elizabeth is head of a leadership team in a large multinational beverage company.

Context A major multi-national beverage company employing 900 people had a national marketing division that had quite a lot of autonomy in marketing different products to the local market but, of course, depended on the brand image to promote sales.

Issue The brand was losing market share. Analysis of the strategic priorities showed that there was a lack of innovation around new products, markets and customers.

Solution Elizabeth and her leadership team ran a set of diagnostics on each individual in the team to discover their competencies and mindset around innovation. The diagnostics showed that the prevailing mindset in the team was risk averse. This was a major eye opener and it enabled Elizabeth to make a decision to recruit someone in with the appropriate mindset and skills to lead innovation.

There is now a company-wide innovation programme and innovative results.

Learning Continuous review of people's competencies and attitudes allows you to keep up with changes in the market and customers' expectations.

Audit summary

Take a few minutes to reflect on the leadership–team effectiveness matrix below and consider your current position: where are you now and what are the implications?

→ Bottom left – poor leadership and an ineffective team will result in failure. Who knows, you may already be too late.

→ Top left – great leadership but a poor team implies that you have a great vision but you will be unlikely to implement it and so it will have little impact. You will need to find a way of developing and motivating the team, and introducing systems and processes to improve team effectiveness.

→ Bottom right – poor leadership but a great team implies you are highly effective and efficient as a team but may well be going in the wrong direction. It is no use being the most innovative and efficient developers of cassettes if everyone has changed to CDs!

→ Top right – clear leadership and direction combined with an efficient and effective team: in effect a high-performing team. This is where we want to be. Lots of great new ideas for improvement linked to current business goals and with a team unit capable of delivering on time and within budget. You don't need this book; please give it to someone else!

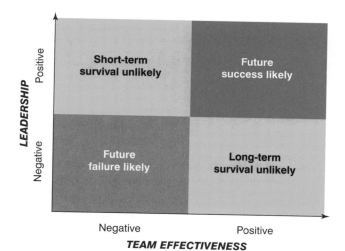

STOP – THINK – ACT

At the end of the individual and team audits take time to reflect on your profile in order to identify any quick wins you could achieve by making changes today, and to read the rest of the book. Look for other areas where you could get a 'quick win' and improve matters in the short term. Ask yourself and the team these questions:

What should we do?	What will you change today, and what difference will it make (why)? How will we know if it has been successful?
Who do we need to involve?	Who else needs to be involved to make it work and why?
What resources will we require?	What information, facilities, materials, equipment or budget will be required and are they available?
What is the timing?	When will this change be implemented – is there a deadline?

Visit **www.Fast-Track-Me.com** to use the FastTrack online planning tool.

EXPERT VOICE

Generation Y and Z: Who are they? Should we manage them differently?

Dr Lynn Thurloway and Dr Jean-Anne Stewart
Henley Business School, University of Reading

Attracting, retaining and motivating people to add value to the organisation is a critical challenge for both managers and organisations. Whilst the general importance of these activities cannot be denied, the emerging generational imbalances and labour market mismatches mean attracting and retaining younger workers becomes more critical and challenges current people management practices. There is currently over 55 per cent of the workforce aged over 45 and only 15 per cent in the Generation Y age group, so we are drawing on a smaller and smaller pool of young talented people, with an ever-increasing older workforce.

Generational research could help you in developing greater understanding of younger workers who have recently entered, or are soon to enter, the workplace. At the heart of this research is the concept that formative events and socialisation develop general values, aspirations and goals that define each generation and influence their behaviour and attitudes, not only to life generally but also to work. Today, the focus of this research is on generation Gen Y (those born between 1980 and 1994) and the generation that follows, Gen Z (those born after 1994), who are just starting to enter the workforce and are particularly prevalent in the retail and catering sectors. There is some confusion between different bodies on the exact age boundaries, but these categories seem to reflect the majority.

So what are the defining features of Gen Y and Z? Research tells us, perhaps not surprisingly, that these generations have been hugely impacted by the rapid technological developments of the past decades, so they are comfortable with technology, social networks and communication, used to multitasking, and are at ease with the wider world and global labour markets. In terms of personal characteristics, the educated Gen Y and Z who are likely to become your core talent of the future have tended to be brought up in non-traditional, often small families, with high levels of parental engagement in every aspect of their lives, high levels of support in education and recognition as an achiever regardless of how small the actual achievement. They like to work in groups and on projects and look for early responsibility supported by lots of feedback. This has led to Gen Y and Z being described as the 'WE' generations. Key personal characteristics include that they are self-motivated, focused on their own careers and comfortable with being mobile, and moving jobs if it contributes to their personal development and careers. They tend to focus on the 'best deal' in terms of rewards and pay, although this does not necessarily mean the highest pay. So they are both self-sufficient and independent and yet happy to work in teams. It is also suggested that work–life balance is important to them but unlike previous generations, where work intruded into home life and people embraced a long hours culture, Gen Y and Z are more likely, especially through social networking (Web 2.0) to bring their social life into work, prompting one commentator[1] to coin the phrase 'plorking', play-working, where they socialise and have fun at work.

Identifying key characteristics of young talent is all very well but what does this mean for you and your organisation? As labour markets tighten, there are likely to be increasing demographic mismatches in many parts of the world, so you are going to have to manage the retention of your key young talent quite carefully. Why? Because the indications are that they are likely to be more impatient with managers and employers if they are not recognised or offered what they want fairly quickly. They have the confidence, self-assurance and ability to organise themselves effectively, through their often large networks, and are prepared to use them! There have been cases where they have left organisations because colleagues were made redundant, even when they were reassured that their own jobs were secure – they had not liked how colleagues were treated, so they moved on. They expect a supportive style of management that allows them independence and responsibility quite early in their careers. So coaching, mentoring and peer learning groups are likely to be more appropriate than more traditional management development approaches. There are also signs that as Gen Y become core to labour markets and Gen Z begin to join, managers and organisations will need to re-evaluate entrenched approaches to managing people and HR processes, if they are to compete effectively for the best talent. Indeed, if Gen Y and Z do fit the generational portrait currently painted, organisations and managers will need to develop styles and HR processes that demonstrate that the Gen Y and Z employee is recognised as central to adding value in the coming years. Gen Y see their future career path as a spider's web, not a ladder, and this will challenge us all!

---

[1] Redmond, P. (Undated) 'Generation Y: Graduates Who Dare to Demand More', *University of Liverpool News*.

PART B

BUSINESS FAST TRACK

rrespective of your chosen function or discipline, look around at the successful managers who you know and admire. We call these people Fast Track managers, people who have the knowledge and skills to perform well and fast track their careers. Notice how they excel at three things:

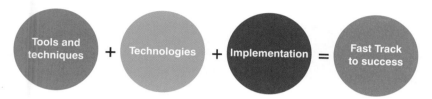

Tools and techniques

They have a good understanding of best practices for their particular field. This is in the form of methods and techniques that translate knowledge into decisions, insights and actions. They understand what the best companies do and have an ability to interpret what is relevant for their own businesses. The processes they use are generally simple to explain and form a logical step-by-step approach to solving a problem or capturing data and insights. They also encourage creativity – Fast Track managers do not follow a process slavishly where they know they are filling in the boxes rather than looking for insights on how to improve performance. This combination of method and creativity produces the optimum solutions.

They also have a clear understanding of what is important to know and what is simply noise. They either know this information or have it at their fingertips as and when they require it. They also have effective filtering mechanisms so that they don't get overloaded with extraneous information. The level of detail required varies dramatically from one situation to another – the small entrepreneur will work a lot more on the knowledge they have and in gaining facts from quick conversations with experts, whereas a large corporate may employ teams of analysts and research companies. Frequently when a team is going through any process, they uncover the need for further data.

Technologies

However, having the facts and understanding best practice will achieve little unless they are built into the systems that people use on a day-to-day basis. Fast Track managers are good at assessing the relevance of new information technologies and adopting the appropriate ones in order to maximise both effectiveness and efficiency.

Implementation

Finally, having designed the framework that is appropriate to them and their team, Fast Track managers have strong influencing skills and are also great at leading the implementation effort, putting in place the changes necessary to build and sustain the performance of the team.

How tightly or loosely you will use the various tools and techniques presented in Part B will vary, and will to a certain extent depend on personal style. As you read through the following three chapters, first seek to understand how each could impact you and your team, and then decide what level of change may be appropriate given your starting point, authority and career aspirations.

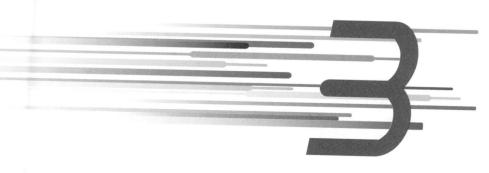

FAST TRACK TOP TEN

This chapter presents a framework of methods or techniques to improve performance and make life as a team manager easier. Each function can take a lifetime to master, but the Fast Track manager will know which areas to focus on – get those areas right and the team will be high performers. Often success relates to the introduction of simple tools and techniques to improve effectiveness and efficiency.

Introducing people and performance management tools and techniques

What needs to be included? – the top ten tools and techniques

Developing a high-performing team comes from a series of steps. These steps are aimed at narrowing down exactly what the team is trying to achieve until the actions listed in the last one are easily measurable and give the whole team coordinated focus. Within the area of people and performance management, the 'top ten' tools and techniques are reflected in the following components:

1 **The vision thing:** Starting with a clear strategic framework.

2 **Business DNA:** Producing performance scorecards and key performance indicators (KPIs). Having set the long-term goals and

strategy for the team you now need to think about the actual composition of the team and how its structure encourages team members to agree what needs to be done, balancing the competencies and specialisations of the people in the team to achieve the common goal.

3 **High-performance teams:** Setting structure, agreeing plans, balancing the team. But, as I have said, team members may be equal leaders in their own specific skills but some, as they say, will be more equal than others. Some, in short, will have the competencies, attitude, talents and strengths to make them key drivers of the team's success. I call these people 'A' players; so find out who they are and help them to become even better.

4 **'A' players:** Identifying key contributors, developing leadership and managing talent. Right, you've developed a high-performing team now let's think about timescale. How long do you want this team to continue to perform excellently? The answer is – for ever. Create a plan that ensures continuity of people and their skills who will take over when team members, for whatever reason, move or are promoted. 'A' players are going to be in demand in your part of the business and in others.

5 **Business continuity:** Succession planning and managing risk. You are going to find that achieving excellent performance requires the people in the team to change how they proceed and behave. Some of them will do it easily, others will require a bit of persuasion, training or whatever it takes. All the members of your team need to develop and improve to match the changing business and industry environment and their career aspirations. This all needs a plan.

6 **Motivating personal change of behaviour:** Getting to 'status Green' through continuous innovation and improvement.

7 **Developing people:** Personal profiling, coaching and personal development planning. Now ask yourself why the team was not high-performing before. High-performing behaviour, we have said, has to stick and become the norm. This will need a cultural

change and a tool to help achieve that. Included in that culture is compliance with the law, the use of best practices and regular review to make sure you are still on track.

8 **Right behaviours/right attitudes:** Changing the organisation's culture to influence the way people act and think.

9 **Effective governance:** Compliance, best practice and perform-ance review meetings. Regular review involves having quick and easy access to information on current, past and forecast per-formance. You need to know how you are doing and, because you're an ambitious team leader, you need other people to be aware of how your performance is improving and developing.

10 **Gaining visibility:** Setting up the leadership dashboard.

1 THE VISION THING

Definitions

A **vision** is a statement of possibility for the business, an aspiration, for example:

→ Company X's vision statement: 'To lead the passionate crea-tion of exceptional drinks at the edge of contemporary culture.'

→ Company Y's vision statement: 'To create a world in which global organisations get their results through leadership that is capable, confident and innovative.'

The vision needs to be framed in words that engage the hearts and minds of the people in the business without too much translation.

A **mission** speaks to the purpose of the organisation, function, division or team in relation to the vision. In other words, the mission is the frame of reference that will define the key actions that will contribute to the achieve-ment of the vision (e.g. 'Elevating social moments around the world'):

→ Company X's mission statement: 'We will establish a culture that reflects the brands.'

→ Company Y's mission statement: 'We will enable our clients to bring their big ideas to life.'

A mission frames the purpose of each of the various elements of an organisation using words that are powerful, meaningful and again engage the hearts and minds of each person.

Vision and mission together provide the context in which to establish the **strategic priorities** for the business. A strategic priority is an area of activity that is key to the fulfilment of the vision. In the example above (to lead the passionate creation of exceptional drinks at the edge of contemporary culture) a strategic priority is: 'To create exceptional brands.'

The logic is that if you do not create exceptional brands how will you be able to fulfil the vision?

Shared **goals** are those target results that are relevant to delivering on the strategic priorities and are a shared responsibility across the business. Define goals in the short, medium and long term, moving towards the vision. Once shared goals have been agreed, then each function can be clear about how to go about establishing its own role with specific goals aligned to the company's goals.

How does a team get from the vision to an action plan?

Start with a clear understanding of the company vision and strategic framework

First define the company vision and strategic framework (characterised by vision, mission and strategic priorities). This is key to enabling the whole organisation to align and is the responsibility of the board or top team to establish.

The best way to achieve the definition of the company's shared goals is to run a company-wide planning session that includes all members of the leadership teams covering all the functions; this can be between 35–50 people. Each team leader can be a sponsor or leader of a cross-functional team working on one of the strategic priorities to establish the short-, medium- and long-term goals. These are verified and/or modified by the other members of the leadership community. In this way members of the leadership community are involved and participate in the creation of shared goals.

Ask: how do I fit and what do I want my team to have as its main purpose or mission?

In order to align your team with the company's strategic framework, facilitate your team through a similar process to the one above. You and your team need to know what the mission for the team is in relation to the function's mission and the company's vision. Make sure that your team buy into the mission and goals by involving them in creating the framework; it could be a team or a whole function's team. What is your team required to deliver and what is the purpose of your team in relation to the company's vision and the function's mission? Make sure that you and the team define this in simple and powerful words that engage members.

Be clear about priorities for the team in relation to company priorities

Take each of the company's strategic priorities and have a team conversation about what these mean to your team. How do they translate? Get the team to associate with the team mission and priorities – making them feel part of the process as they work towards shared goals, then check team goals for congruence with the company's financial goals.

Identify the key actions that define the short-term goals for each company strategic priority area

The figure on page 36 is an example of a vision to action plan.

QUICK TIP **STRATEGIC FRAMEWORK**
Get the team to take responsibility for summarising the strategic framework as a charter on one sheet of paper. Distribute the charter to all levels in the company. You would send it to your regional manager, marketing teams, finance and operations. You want all areas of the business that you interact with to understand what you are aiming for.

CONCEPT	FEATURES
Vision or aspiration	Highly ambiguous generalisation for an aspiration of who or what the business can aspire to
Mission or purpose	In relation to the vision • Ambiguous • Generates emotional buy-in • Provides direction to the overall style activity in moving towards the aspiration • Describes the purpose of a team in relation to the aspiration
Strategic priorities	• Those mission critical areas from which the shared goals are identified and agreed, e.g. organisational capability, customers, innovation, stakeholders, etc.
Long-term goal *(to be time relevant)*	• Moderate between ambiguous and specific • Time bound • Move the organisation towards the delivery of the vision/mission
Medium-term goal	• Time-bound • Move the goal towards delivery of long-term goal
Short-term goal	• 12-month period – specific to the next 12 months and supports medium-term goals
Imperatives	• Key top priorities required to deliver short-term goal • Provides the short-term leadership focus
Initiatives	• New activities that enable the team in creating the future
Action	Highly specific, detailed tasks that deliver on imperatives and are executed by teams through the organisation

2 BUSINESS DNA

Business DNA is a term used to describe the mechanism or 'blueprint' that links all aspects of the organisation to the others, and to its vision and mission. Many organisations often implement the strategy of the business badly, if at all. Whilst the strategic thinking by the leadership team may have been sound and relevant, people up and down the business often fail to understand what it really means, how well they are implementing it or even how it impacts them on a day-to-day basis. This can result at best in operational inefficiency, and at worst in a complete failure to change the business in line with market expectations. This finally leads to loss of competitiveness.

Make sure you close this critical gap and embed strategic decisions in daily routines.

How do I do that?

Use key performance indicators (KPIs) as the mechanism to link the top-level vision for the business down to the individual drivers of performance on a day-to-day basis.

When you have made a start by reviewing the vision, mission and goals for the business and translated them into a strategic framework (vision, mission and goals) for your team, review your thinking with your manager. Use the opportunity to clarify any concerns or open items you may have, i.e. areas that are not fully understood. Then spend time with your colleagues in other functions or teams to check that there is no duplication or gap. Finally, review your strategic framework with your team, asking members to critically review your work, so that they understand the implications for each of them and identify any potential problems with the implementation.

After that, translate your team goals into a series of KPIs – ask yourself how you will monitor progress and success. Ensure that you have between four and ten KPIs to make up your 'performance scorecard' that meet the following criteria:

→ Each KPI is aligned to the overall company and team strategic frameworks, and in total they make up a balanced set of financial and non-financial indicators, and current and predictive indicators. Note that many organisations now use four categories of KPI to provide what is called a 'balanced scorecard' based on: financial results, customer and brand, operational effectiveness, and learning and growth.[1] Ensure your KPIs also fit together as a set and that they do not conflict with one another or with KPIs in another team or at another level – this is sometimes referred to as the 'golden thread'.

[1] Kaplan, R. and Norton, D. (1992) 'The Balanced Scorecard – Measures that Drive Perfromance', *Harvard Business Review*, February.

→ Each KPI is SMART: **specific** and clearly defined; **measurable** so that you can check on a regular basis how you are performing; **achievable** so that each KPI provides a target that is stretching but not so extreme that it is no longer motivational; **relevant** to your team and what it is aiming to achieve; and **time bound** in terms of deadlines or timing for when each KPI will be achieved.

→ Each KPI has clear targets so that over- and under-performance can be identified easily and flagged for review. Be clear about when and how often each is to be reviewed – typically weekly or monthly. Whilst you may monitor hard numbers, get into the habit of presenting data in a simple-to-understand format such as using a Red (immediate corrective action is required), Amber (some concerns and needs to be monitored closely) and Green (on-track) colour coding. Think also about how and when poor performance in any area should be escalated to a higher level.

The figure opposite is an example of a team scorecard with Red-Amber-Green indicators.

QUICK TIP *KEY PERFORMANCE INDICATORS*
Keep your set of KPIs simple and easy to measure. Then use them to drive your regular (monthly) performance review meetings.

Once your balanced scorecard is defined and reflects your team success factors or business DNA, validate that it is correct by testing it with historic and current data. KPIs are used to trigger reviews leading to assessment of cause and corrective action – ask yourself what you would have done differently had you had this scorecard for your past few performance review meetings.

Finally, do not expect perfection from day one. Developing a balanced set of KPIs can take time, and it often takes at least three performance review cycles before the process starts to work. So in this initial phase, be prepared to change the KPIs if they are not right.

Type	Jan	Feb	Mar	Apr	May	Jun	Jul	Aug	Sep	Oct	Nov	Dec	Issues
Benefits realisation	Red	Amb	Amb	Red	Red	Red	Red	Red	Red	Red			8
Customer satisfaction and relationship	Amb	Amb	Amb	Gre	Gre	Gre	Gre	Gre	Amb	Red			3
Delivery excellence	Gre	Gre	Gre	Gre	Gre	Red	Red	Red	Red	Red			4
Financial health	Red	Amb	Amb	Red	Red	Red	Amb	Red	Red	Red			6
Innovation growth and learning	Red	Gre	Gre	Gre	Gre	Gre	Gre	Gre	Gre	Gre			3
Production services	Gre	Gre	Gre	Amb	Amb	Amb	Amb	Amb	Red	Red			8

Overall totals

	Jan	Feb	Mar	Apr	May	Jun	Jul	Aug	Sep	Oct	Nov	Dec	Issues
	Red	Amb	Amb	Red	Red	Red	Red	Red	Red	Red			32

3 HIGH-PERFORMANCE TEAMS

High-performance **teams** are essential in creating a high-performing organisation. High-performing organisations are not achieved through high-performing **individuals**: it is the sum of the individual team members that creates a level of performance that is greater than the whole team. You develop high-performance teams through time. High performance is a state that lies beyond the achievement of numeric goals and contains the ingredients for sustainable high performance through time.

All teams go through four development phases commonly referred to as: forming, storming, norming and performing. These development phases can be accelerated through team development programmes. (There is more detail on these phases in Chapter 7, Leading the team.)

The faster you can get your team to a high-performing state the better and more consistent your results will be. You will also become less dependent on individual high performers, rather on high performers operating in a cohesive, collaborative and unified team where the power of the whole team is much greater than the individual performances. Teams that are dependent on individual high performers have a tendency to be dysfunctional, suffer performance peaks and troughs, low morale and inconsistent results. Members of high-performing teams know how to complement each other's skills and act in a unified cohesion of those skills to get optimal results or outcomes.

How do I do this?

High performance means the achievement of results, through the best use of the team's skills, talents and personalities.

→ Create a benchmark (internally and externally) to measure against. Katzenbach and Smith[2] recognise that many managers and business leaders do not have a clear understanding of the stages of team development and therefore miss the performance potential within existing teams, failing to identify new team

[2] Katzenbach, J.R. and Smith, D.K. (1993) *The Wisdom of Teams*, Boston, MA: Harvard Business School Press.

opportunities. They created a simple set of benchmarks for building high-performing teams in which they suggest that the following dimensions are key:

→ The team has an overriding sense of purpose.
→ The team builds on the strengths and skills of the individuals within it.
→ There is a strong results ethic.
→ There is open communication and mutual accountability (joint responsibility in delivering a result).
→ The team is cohesive, compassionate, concerned for the welfare of individual team members and unified. In this context cohesive means emotional – it sticks together through adversity (i.e. good and bad times) and members commit to each other. It is unified in relation to common business objectives and outcomes.
→ The team has a unique social system.

This is shown in our figure below.

1. Overwhelming sense of purpose	% score
2. Builds on strengths and skills	% score
3. Strong results ethic	% score
4. Open communication and accountability	% score
5. Cohesive, compassionate and unified	% score
6. Unique social system	% score

What do you need to change to get to 100%?

→ Make sure you have a clear strategic framework that provides the overall direction for the team. Within this structure clarify the roles and responsibilities of each team member and ensure consistency with best practices. Make sure that individual roles are aligned with the core processes that are essential to delivering consistent results.

→ Understand what talent is required and what you have. Then define how talent will be used in terms of delivering against shared goals. For example, if you have someone who comes up with great ideas, involve them at the stage where you are defining the best way to achieve the goal. If you have someone who is talented at delivery, have them play a central role in execution of the tasks necessary to deliver the result. You may have someone who is great at building and retaining relationships, so use them to help you manage the key stakeholders.

→ Teams are made up of individuals with different personalities. It's very often the case that conflict and dysfunctional behaviour will break out among team members because they don't understand how to work with each other and value other team members' differences. Make sure that you have a good balance of different personalities, otherwise you may get skews that are disempowering and counterproductive. Here are a couple of examples:

  → A team in a national operation which was part of a major drinks manufacturer had 80 per cent of the team members risk averse. They found that the major requirement going forward was innovation. There is skew here that will prevent the team from succeeding.

  → A senior team in a major pharmaceutical company was unable to bring new ideas to life. The majority of the team members were good at conceiving new ideas. They did not recognise or value the talent of one of its team members who was able to put structure around ideas and define actions to bring them to life.

There are numerous web-based tools that will enable you to identify the personality types of each of the team members and provide a background to the deployment of the team members. This enables you and them to achieve an understanding of how best to deploy people, build effective working relationships and communicate more easily with them.

By using these tools you can define the traits of each member of your team. If you then run team building sessions you can ensure people can work effectively together, given the diversity and contribution of each player in the team.

QUICK TIP **KEEP LOOKING FOR BALANCE**
Make sure that there is an even distribution of people with the personality styles of risk appetite and risk aversion.

4 'A' PLAYERS

We are all operating in an environment where companies small and large are competing with each other on a global scale. This has been made possible through developing technologies that enable businesses to service customers and consumers globally without the need to leave the country. There is increasing competition for highly capable, talented people. Your ability to compete for them effectively depends to a large extent on what level of people management skills you have. With this in mind, the art of identifying capable people, utilising them, rewarding them and keeping them interested has turned into both an art and a science. Large organisations build talent management systems and bring specialists on board whose sole responsibility is to put a system in place to manage and maintain an organisation's talent.

With increasing global competition for people, make sure you keep your key people. To do this, move them into bigger roles and increase their leadership or management responsibilities. To sustain the business and be able to fill the gaps left behind if key people do leave requires planning and decisions about who could fill those gaps. Firstly, you need to know that the individual taking over is capable, that they have the right skills to fulfil the role and that their talents or strengths are suitable for the position.

The world is full of dissatisfied people, round pegs in square holes who at best deliver a passable result but who are never going to thrive and excel in the roles they are put into. People are often put into roles that don't suit them, either through ignorance or simply because it's expedient: you need the job done and they need the job.

What are 'A' players?

Bradford Smart in his book *Topgrading*[3] suggests that a key ingredient in building high-performing teams is to ensure that 70 per cent of your team is comprised of 'A' Players, 30 per cent 'B' players and no 'C' players. This is based upon your company's ability to hire the best that you can afford to pay for, and your location or the location of the job you want the 'A' person to do.

'A' players are people with a high level of competence in those competencies required for the role. Whether a person can be classified as 'A' material is role dependent and also context-dependent. In other words, if you promote a person who is an 'A' performer in a sales role, it does not follow that they will be 'A' in a sales management role.

A board level financial director from a big, fast-moving consumer goods (FMCG) company was headhunted into a financial director role with a large hedge funds company. The hedge funds company was growing exponentially, investment decisions were made at the speed of light – a very different environment to the slow, steady one of the huge FMCG company. This very successful senior 'A' player could not make the context change fast enough to be able to perform as an 'A' player and rapidly became a 'C' player who lasted six months.

Competence (skills)

Bradford Smart suggests that there are two dimensions to 'A' players. The first dimension is **competence (skills)** in a role. Be very clear about the skills that are required in each role within your team.

---

[3] Smart, B. (2005) *Topgrading: how leading companies win by hiring, coaching and keeping the best people*, Portfolio.

→ An 'A' player is someone who exceeds expectations in 50 per cent or more of the skills required to do the role.

→ A 'B' player is one who is good to very good in 50 per cent or more of the skills required to do the role.

→ A 'C' player is below the level of a 'B' player and is someone who is good/average in 50 per cent or more of the skills. The role of 'C' players is to support 'B' players. You would not have 'C' players in leadership roles in your high-performing team.

Attitude

The second dimension is **attitude**. A positive attitude towards the job, the company, work colleagues and customers will give you an 'A+' distinction. A negative attitude will give you an 'A−' distinction. In the case of an 'A−' it may be appropriate to put this person into a role where they can act largely on their own to get the results or, if they need to interact with others, that you are very clear with them about their need to change their attitude.

Talents or strengths

The third dimension is the dimension of a person's strengths and talent: those things that a person is excellent at, that lie either within the skills set required or, as is very often the case, outside and beyond those skills. People are at their most productive, engaged and content when applying their talent. Here are three examples:

→ A person may have a talent for delivering. They deliver exceptional results, to budget, to deadline consistently and quite naturally.

→ A person that is able to build relationships with anyone quickly and easily in a way that is sustainable has a great talent.

→ A talented person may be able to take complex ideas and translate them into everyday language and actions that others can follow.

How do I apply this framework?

Step one: Set objectives and identify required results

Be very clear about your team's objectives. What are the results you need to deliver consistently to fulfil your objectives? What is your team's mission or purpose?

A well-formed outcome based on clear objectives sets the context for identifying the required skill sets. You need to answer the following questions:

1 What is it your team needs to achieve (specific, measurable, agreed, realistic and time-bound)?

2 What are the benefits to the business in achieving this outcome with your team?

3 Where are you and your team now in relation to achieving this outcome?

4 What does success look like? What are you and your team delivering in order to achieve this outcome? What are the internal measures and what are the external measures? (What do your customers and stakeholders consider to be the criteria for your success?)

5 What is the first thing you need to do to achieve this outcome?

6 What are the main milestones or steps towards achieving this outcome?

7 What resources (e.g. people, skills, investment) are required to fulfil this outcome?

8 What resources do you have now that will enable you to fulfil the outcome?

9 What is the deadline for delivering this outcome?

Step two: Identify skill sets

→ Identify tasks that are 'mission critical'.

→ Highlight specific technical skill sets required.

→ Assess the support required, e.g. administration, secretarial, etc.

→ What level of competence is required to fulfil each task area – high, medium or low?

→ Define the roles of people in the team.

→ Define key accountabilities: what are the deliverables that each person will be held responsible for?

→ Which roles are 'A' player roles? (Mission critical roles that deliver mission critical activities.)

→ Which are the 'B' player roles? (Support and other activities surrounding mission critical activity.)

A competency framework example, in this case for an 'A' player, is shown here.

Leadership Summary Page: Rating (A) PLayer   **Name:** Steve Apple

Competence	Poor	Good	Very good	Excellent
Concept formation				90%
Strategic thinking				85%
Decision making – Quality – Speed				80%
Influence		60%		
Communication – Spoken – Written			75%	
Stakeholder management				80%
Collaboration				92%
Business building			70%	

In a well-known spirits company that had a marketing team of six players, there were three 'A' players, two 'B' players and one 'C' player at the team-forming stage. Performance was average and particularly poor in the innovation area for a period of a year. After this the leadership of the team was changed and one of the 'A' players took over as leader. The new leader restructured the team moving out one 'B' player and a 'C' player, and bringing in an 'A' player. The team has seen a quantum shift in results and has an ambitious programme for innovation now in place. The leader did this by going through the steps needed to identify the status of each team member.

QUICK TIP *BE OBJECTIVE*
Leave emotions and loyalties out of your evaluation of player capabilities. The lack of sufficient 'A' player capability will seriously handicap your team's performance.

5 BUSINESS CONTINUITY

Business continuity is about being able to sustain the business through time. People change their ambitions and as a consequence will leave to satisfy those ambitions elsewhere. The organisation needs to change according to the business climate and the external landscape. Leave yourself with options and enough flexibility to handle growth and change. Business continuity means planning for this growth and change, and always having the right people resources at the right time.

Being able to flex and change means being able to replace people from within because often that is the fastest way of ensuring that you have replacements that can be up to speed quickly. It's generally a faster option than going through the recruitment process and training from scratch.

Make sure that you are paying people the right amount of money compared to what they could get from your competitors. You must understand the importance of being able to keep people engaged and motivated to stay in the business as opposed to finding another job with the competition.

Succession planning

Succession planning is an art and a science that requires some thought and an understanding of what you will need in terms of skills and talent for the future. It requires you to use your strategic plan as a road map for determining what skills and talents are needed in two to three years' time in relation to what your team will need to be able to produce at that time.

You need to understand what resource and potential you have now and make some choices about whom you will be developing to succeed the various mission critical roles you will have in the future. You may develop some of your team members by moving them into different roles around the business; so you need to be aware of those opportunities too.

Succession planning starts with a regular review of your map of the future:

→ What skills/talent do you have now and what will you need in 18 months to two years? Remember that it will take you six months to do a search to recruit someone and six months to get them on board.

→ Who has the potential to be developed into new mission critical roles in the required timeframe?

→ Identify one person on your team who could be developed to succeed each of your present mission critical roles.

Risk register

Your risk register should contain a list of people with skills and relationships that are highly sought after by your competitors. It is important to have a constant dialogue with these individuals, particularly when your business may be going through a tough time or a new company comes on to the competitive scene.

People who have come from a competitor could be at risk if they are not integrated properly into your culture.

Staff retention starts from good knowledge of your industry:

→ Understand how well you are positioned against your competitors. People like to work for winners and you will find that you need to find other factors to keep your best people on board when your business is going through a downturn.

→ Make sure you understand where you stand in the competitive pay stakes.

→ Make sure you understand people's needs, values and ambitions. What do they want in their life? If you can't help them achieve those things, then you won't be able to keep them.

Use a risk matrix such as the one opposite to identify people you are at risk of losing. For each dimension think about the probability (P) that there is a problem, the level of impact (I) if there is a problem, and the overall risk factor (P × I). Consider:

→ Compensation – is it competitive to retain their services?

→ Strategic thinking – is the person's thinking in line with current and future strategy?

→ Decision making – is the level of responsibility and authority appropriate to the person's experience?

→ Cultural fit – is there alignment between the values of the business, the team and the person?

→ Personal aspirations – can the person achieve their personal goals within the team and business?

→ Technical skills – does the person have the necessary technical skills to do a great job?

In the following risk diagram, team risks are shown in a two-dimensional matrix (Probability × Impact)

Risk Matrix

Name: _____   **Position:** _____

Competence	Probability		Impact		Risk	
	High	Low	High	Low	High	Low
1. Compensation						
2. Strategic thinking						
3. Decision making						
4. Cultural fit						
5. Personal aspirations						
6. Demand for technical skill						

Probability = probablility of risk in the particular dimension (1–6)
Impact = impact on the individual of a mismatch in 1–6
Risk = overall risk rating per dimension

Here are some examples:

→ An investment bank once headhunted and recruited a whole team from a competitor to join its equities research division. The cost of recruiting the whole team cost millions. After two months the entire team left and went back to the original bank due to a mismatch in culture and values.

→ One day at the beginning of a new budget year, a divisional director of an investment bank came into the office and found his two best managers waiting for him. Both of them resigned taking with them 12 of his best people and with them went their most loyal customers. He had a hole of £20 million before he had even 'opened for business' in his new budget year. Asked the question, 'How did you not know they were at risk?', he replied, 'What do you mean, I'm not sure what you're getting at?' The response to this was, 'Well, did you have a conversation with them about what they wanted in their career, did you find out what was important to them as individuals?' He replied, 'We don't have conversations like that here!'

> **QUICK TIP** *KEEP IN TOUCH WITH YOUR PEOPLE*
> Find out what people want if you don't already know.

A 'conversation' that the divisional manager should have had would look something like this:

→ Ask: 'What do you want to achieve in the next 12 months in your career?'

→ Following the response, ask: 'What is important to you about that?' The first question will get you the person's goal; the second question will get you one value.

→ Repeat the 'What's important' question twice more until you have three values.

→ Repeat the above process to find out what the mid-term career goal is and the values associated with that.

Finally, ask yourself whether those goals are realistically achievable in your team or business.

6 MOTIVATING PERSONAL CHANGE OF BEHAVIOUR

Your ability to motivate individuals in the team to change is a critical success factor in building a high-performance team. Providing structure and direction are vital ingredients to high-performing teams. Motivation to change is the only way to generate behaviour changes in teams and individuals. Unless an individual feels the desire to change, they are unlikely to be able change their behaviour with any degree of sustainability. Human beings are wedded to habitual ways of behaving, the roots of which lie far back in time. These behaviours are ingrained and unconscious, and can often derail a team's performance. Assisting individuals to change these behaviours requires an ability to work with them to understand what their personal goals, values and aspirations are.

Change in teams and organisations can be completely sabotaged by first-order learning, which is the long-held beliefs and behaviours established over the life of the individual. Second-order learning, which is what the team leader is trying to promote here, challenges these deeply held beliefs and behaviours through motivation to change.

This is how to go about it.

Reinforce the need to change and be specific about what is required

The first step in generating behavioural change is to give the individual very specific feedback about the behaviour they need to change. For example, to someone missing deadlines consistently: 'I want to give you some feedback about your performance on "X" task. You achieve very high-quality presentation in your reports. They are always numerically accurate and written very clearly. The one thing that you need to change is that your reports always miss the deadline we have agreed. That is causing problems in my being able to meet my commitments to my boss and to the organisation. Overall, your work is excellent.'

Calibrate their current motivation to change

Are they really motivated or just playing at it? People receive feedback personally and so the way you give feedback is important. Notice their reaction by observing body language and the words they respond with. If they are not congruent you need to pursue this further. The likelihood of change is remote unless you can see and sense real motivation to make the change.

Discuss their personal values and personal career goals

This should be done for the short and medium term. Motivation to change is very personal. Change takes energy and effort and human beings are designed to take the path of least resistance. Unless a person can make a connection with what's in it for them they won't feel that the change is worth the effort, consciously or unconsciously. You need to find out more about them personally.

Talk about what they want to achieve in their career in the short and medium term. Once you understand their goals, find out what is important to them about those goals: 'What is important to you about achieving goal X?' Now you have two goals and up to six values. (Values are normally couched in terms like success, status, money, freedom or independence.)

Create a contrast frame if they do not change

Once you have the two goals and six values, create a contrast frame in which you take the behaviour they need to change and ask what impact there will be on each goal and each value in turn if they do change the behaviour and/or if they don't change the behaviour. The person's brain will be able to make conscious distinctions about whether or not the change is going to have a positive or negative impact on what is important to them.

Confirm the motivation to change

Alternatively, agree that the person is not motivated because change does not fit their needs and then agree alternatives.

The following motivation to change model is based on the question: 'What is the behaviour they need to develop in order to get the desired result, instead of the behaviour they are currently using that is not getting the desired result?'

CASE STORY *INCONGRUENT PERSONAL AND ORGANISATIONAL GOALS, ANDREW'S STORY*

Narrator Andrew was an investment banker in charge of 300 researchers operating in ten teams.

Context Andrew received feedback that he needed to give performance feedback and coach his people to higher levels of performance.

Issue He was not particularly motivated to get involved with people to that degree. His ten-year goal was to be able to make sufficient money from shares in the bank to be able to buy a tract of forest in the Amazon. (He was an ecologist at heart.) This meant that his mid-term goal was to be promoted to the European board and be granted shares.

The short-term goal was to achieve his financial targets consistently through his direct reports to whom he would delegate so that he could spend more time on strategic activity and building relationships with senior people in the bank. His values were: success, financial security, achievement and making a difference.

Solution Andrew's boss went through the questions involved In the motivation to change model. When examining what impact the behaviour change would have on his goals and values Andrew became consciously aware that none of his goals were achievable unless he did make the change.

Learning If you do not know the person well enough to understand their personal goals and values, they will struggle to change their behaviour. Going through the motivation to change model will effectively reveal to you and them whether they will ever make the change. Alternatively they could become determined to make the change because they understand the personal benefits of the change to them as well as to the team and the organisation.

 QUICK TIP *USING PERSONAL GOALS AND VALUES*
Once you have understood the motivation of each team member, write it down and learn how to use this frame consistently when giving feedback and motivating people to change.

7 DEVELOPING PEOPLE

There are two outcomes to bear in mind when making a commitment to develop people. The first is to enable your company or team to achieve its goals. The second is to generate commitment, loyalty and motivation through employee satisfaction. People are more engaged when you take a personal interest in their growth and well-being.

Development means the progressive growth of personal capability through activity that is new in context and the application of skills. This can be achieved by learning through a new set of responsibilities, a new role, a new task, a different culture and through assisting people to change their habitual behaviours.

The steps involved

Identify the behaviours that people need to have in each role to maximise the impact on shared goals of the company and team. In order to be able to calibrate performance, contrast the outcome you require the person to achieve with their current achievements and then think about the behaviour they are currently using. To focus on what people need to develop or change in their behaviour, you need to be clear about what successful behaviours in a role look like. There are a number of ways to achieve this:

1 By looking at competency frameworks produced by professionals for similar teams or organisations and using these as reference material to define the competencies and behaviours for the roles in your team.

2 By referring to your own experience of having been in the roles yourself and modelling on your own experience. Ask, 'What is essential in terms of professional skills? What is essential in terms of supporting core skills?' When you have identified the six to eight key competencies, take it a step further and identify the essential behaviours required to deliver on each competence.

3 Meet each team member and explain the competency framework that applies to them in their role. Invite them to add to or
   modify the required behaviours. Explain that this framework
   will be one dimension of how you will measure their performance, the two other dimensions being the achievement of their
   key performance objectives and their attitude. Ensure that there
   is common understanding about what their overall contribution
   needs to be and how this plays a role in the overarching goals
   of the team.

Check where each member of the team is, and what behaviours they
need to change or develop. Gain agreement from the team member
and ensure they understand both what is required and why.

As you go through the exercise in point 3 above, check that you
know where team members are in terms of their strengths and weaknesses in relation to the framework. Give them the feedback and
ensure that they accept the challenge to develop in the areas of priority.
Make sure that you minimise the amount of change and focus on the
one key thing that will make the greatest difference to their performance
and contribution overall.

Agree personal development plans for each individual: how will
change be effected and what will the specific results and impact be on
performance? Confirm how this will be measured and linked to annual
salary reviews.

Developing performance

Use the following six-step model to developing high performance[4]:

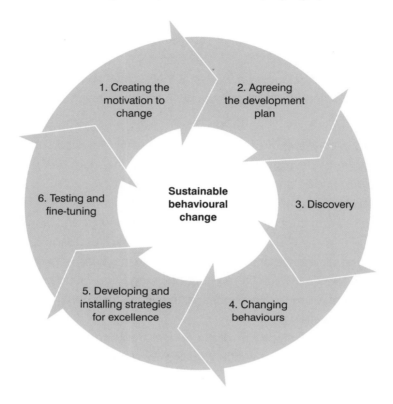

1 Create the motivation to change

Provide the means for people to become committed to changing behaviours and actions to achieve the results you are seeking.

2 Agree the personal development plan

Create a plan that charts the current situation and the specific skills you want and need your team to develop to attain business and team goals.

3 Discovery

Using a wide range of specialist tools and techniques, enable your team to identify and understand the behaviours and beliefs that currently hinder their further development.

[4] Six Steps to Unlimited Performance© Performance Unlimited

4 Changing behaviours

Enable your team to change old behavioural patterns at an unconscious level.

5 Develop and install new strategies for excellence

Design new strategies to go beyond the team's previous best then build them at an unconscious level so that new skills become automatic.

6 Test and fine-tune

Using practical exercises and the feedback gained from them, test the success of new strategies and skills, and refine them to the level of excellence.

Personal development planning

Having given your feedback and gained agreement, check that there is **motivation to change**. Agree a personal development plan and explore options for developing the skills/behaviours. There are many interventions you can offer – training, coaching, action learning and so on.

The outline for a personal development plan is as follows:

→ Confirm what the individual's strengths are and what you want them to focus on.

→ Outline the weaknesses discussed, and confirm the key area for development and change. Be specific about the behaviour currently being used and what the required change in behaviour is.

→ Confirm what success looks like, feels like and sounds like.

→ Confirm what coaching, support, training or action learning experiences you have agreed.

→ Confirm deadlines for the change.

→ Create a coaching culture throughout your team.

→ Encourage everyone on the team to give each other performance-related feedback and to coach each other.

→ Establish a mechanism and timings for regular reviews.

→ Personal development plans should be reviewed once a quarter and updated accordingly.

What follows is a manager's summary of a conversation he has had with a team member regarding the latter's personal development plan:

→ 'You have a natural ability to build relationships with people and fellow team members find you easy to work with. We agreed that this strength will enhance the ability of the team to work together towards shared goals and that you will focus on becoming the glue that pulls the team together so it does a better job of engaging.'

→ 'Don't lose focus on the goal(s). Make a habit of always asking yourself, "What is the purpose of what I am about to do?" before you do anything. This will also give purpose to your relationship building.'

→ 'Stakeholder outcomes will be the acid test of success. Which means you know you're on the right track if your relationships with team members are focused on and driven by those agreed outcomes. As you become more focused, so other team members will become more effective at managing relationships as they model their skills on yours.'

→ 'As we progress I will provide coaching support to help you to focus on outcomes for stakeholder relationships and then review these outcomes with you and the team quarterly.'

→ 'The deadline for having all relevant stakeholder outcomes in place is six months from now.'

QUICK TIP COACHING CULTURE
If you want to establish a coaching culture you will have to demonstrate this consistently every day yourself. Remember that it is important to give feedback also purely in terms of what a person has done well.

8 RIGHT BEHAVIOURS, RIGHT ATTITUDE

It is important that the team is able to 'walk the talk': in other words, to demonstrate collectively and individually the behaviours that produce the desired results. This will generate a model for sustainable best practice and enable other followers and newcomers to quickly understand how to behave.

A term coined for this collective walking the talk is 'a way of being'. A way of being is a habitual set of default behaviours that are unconscious and happen automatically. Human beings are designed to be creatures of habit and so this concept is a natural path for human learning. To form a common way of being requires the team to agree on the values, beliefs and skills that will drive the desired behaviours. A common way of approaching things is an important characteristic when defining a successful team. It also sends a clear message to the rest of the business about how things are to be done. The way of being needs to be aligned to the vision, mission and imperatives so that the habitual behaviours always help lead to those goals.

Without clear guidelines on how to behave people fall back on their personal habits. A way of being is about creating clear guidelines for people to follow.

How do I create a 'way of being'

In order to create a way of being for your team first take the overall strategic framework for the team and ask, 'How does this team need to be to deliver that?' For example: 'Our vision is an organisation that achieves its results through leadership that is capable, confident and informed. Our mission is to enable our clients to bring their big ideas to life: the way of being that makes that possible is the attitude that "we live to inspire, innovate and make a difference in everything that we do".'

Develop a one-line phrase to encapsulate the message for the whole team. Work with your team to agree on the wording. The result will be the team's way of being statement: 'We are a disciplined and flexible team. We make change happen with a common purpose to deliver value.'

Next, break the way of being down into a set of values, beliefs, a state of mind and behaviours that will reinforce the way of being. Assist the team to develop it themselves.

The following diagram is an example of a way of being statement that reflects five core components: values, corresponding and supportive set of beliefs, set of behaviours, set of skills and state of mind (e.g. energetic or calm).

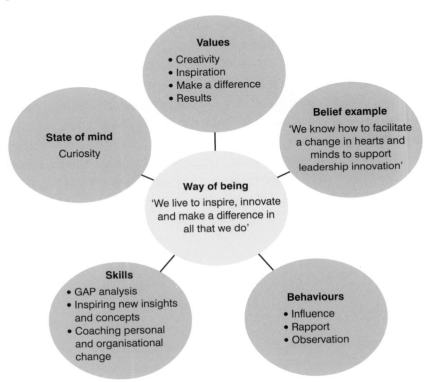

QUICK TIP *EMBEDDING THE 'WAY OF BEING' STATEMENT*

A way of being is an action statement that captures the critical behaviours required to fulfil the vision and mission. Repeat this statement often and in normal conversation with the team to embed it.

9 EFFECTIVE GOVERNANCE

Governance is about measuring how you are doing against the rules of engagement you have established. That applies equally for the business internally as well as for external bodies such as industry standards and operating rules for companies that meet legislative requirements.

Without reviews, you are flying blind and can't take corrective action. Without following externally generated procedures and best practice, your company just won't be seen as being professional. Which means your business will not be able to compete on the same playing field as your competitors.

How do I measure governance

→ Conduct monthly performance review meetings (PRMs) and monitor progress against the strategic framework (your radar screen).

→ In order to keep track of performance and progress against your goals, you will need to review them with your team once a month. This will give you sufficient flexibility to be able to adapt and make corrective changes as required. Monthly review meetings can be conducted using the strategic framework as a radar screen from which to calibrate. Take all your strategic priorities and check that they are still relevant. Market conditions are changing so quickly you can't assume that priorities will stay the same and you may need to change them. Once you have done that quick relevancy check, go through the goals for the short to medium term and check on progress. Do this in a way that team members are contributing, thus reinforcing their involvement and accountability. Then identify areas of concern – Red and Amber status KPIs.

→ Finally, be clear about key corrective actions – who is going to do what, when? Agree and note down any actions arising and the action owners. Publish the actions to all team members following the meeting.

→ Check for compliance with industry standards as well as company rules and regulations (such as budgeting procedures). An additional agenda item for your monthly meetings is to check on any compliance issues/actions and/or operational rules and regulations for the company.

→ Be aware of what your competitors are doing by monitoring industry best practice – keep looking up and out *not* just in and down.

→ Do not become introspective – either when things go well or when they aren't. That's because when things go well there is no pressure to look around for improvements. When things are not going so well there is a tendency to look inwards towards what we know best and try to find familiar solutions such as cost-cutting. What we should do instead is look outwards, examine what the competition is doing and see what opportunities exist for creating new products and services. The most progressive companies constantly monitor and are consistently aware of internal and external opportunities for innovation.

An example

The following example is a plan for a global marketing team's performance review meetings, together with a sample of some of the strategic issues discussed.

Priorities radar screen

The team agreed to develop a priorities radar screen in order to identify:

1 What are the things not getting done and creating bottlenecks?

2 What are the most important things to focus on in the global marketing leadership team (GMLT)?

3 GMLT meetings will run every Friday for three hours and once a month for a full day.

4 Other projects needing to be added to the project's portfolio such as flavours and business as usual.

5 Global marketing initiatives that require team coordination and planning, e.g. presentations on projects N, P and A.

The strategic radar screen acts as a meeting structure for the GMLT. In the following example we can see how the vision and mission are achieved through five strategic priorities. These in turn have been broken into short-terms goals (within one year), specific actions (the 100-day plan and key projects), and an assessment of the impact on key stakeholders. Finally, the team looks internally to assess the state of readiness in terms of the talent and capabilities at hand for success.

PERFORMANCE REVIEW MEETING AGENDA FRAMEWORK

Vision: To create a world in which global organisations get their results through leadership that is confident, capable and informed.
Mission: To assist clients to bring their big ideas to life.

Strategic priorities	Purposeful innovation	Create exceptional brands	Operational excellence	Simple ways of working	Exceptional people and teams
Short-term goal (12 months)	A	B	C	D	E
100-day plan (next 100 days)	XYZ	XYZ	XYZ	XYZ	XYZ
Key projects	Innovation Leadership	Six-step Coaching Model	Program Delivery	Forecasting	Team development programme
Stakeholder impact					
Talent and capability requirement review					
Notes:					
Actions:					
Owner:					

The radar screen features several strategic priorities. The following are examples of **short-term goals** for four out of the five in the previous table:

1 **Purposeful innovation:** 'to bring project "X" and Project "Y" to steering committee approval and gain appropriate investment from the company leadership team'.

2 **Create exceptional brands:** 'to ensure that mission critical projects have "A" players leading them and that each project has a clear strategic framework and project team'.

3 **Operational excellence:** 'to ensure regular communication of priorities and progress on mission critical projects at weekly breakfast meetings'.

4 **Excellent people and teams:** 'to evaluate all employees in global marketing and categorise who are our "A" players, "B" players and "C" Players. Ensure that "A" players are positioned on mission critical activities, "B" players are developed to support the "A" players, and "C" players are developed or moved into more appropriate roles'.

Key projects – guidelines for project management
It was agreed that there was a need to issue a set of project management guidelines. The project planning process will reveal deadlines and decision points that trigger subject and content for global marketing leadership team meetings. It was also agreed that there needs to be a process for evaluating new ideas.

The following are examples of key projects:

→ Resolve the compensation issues and settle the key people who are mission critical. Owners: John/Pete/Andrew (7 February).

→ Generate a repeatable system for project management; be clear about what project managers can decide. Owners: team by next GMT review.

→ Propose company-wide forum for joined up thinking on the three-year plan. Owner: Pete, next leadership team meeting.

→ Resolve our advertising agency contract issues. Owner: Cecelia/Elizabeth (6 March).

→ Brand strategy and communication development. Align with Paris, Tuesday 10 March.

→ Agree and publish principles of working with the local country distributors. Owner: team by 15 April.

→ Finalise the ways of working document for the USA. Owner: Pete, 20 April.

→ Use GMLT appropriately for reviewing all areas of the business, the projects and global company initiatives. Owner: team.

→ GMLT needs to prioritise time and efficient use of resources.

QUICK TIP *TAKE MINUTES*
Get one team member to record regular team minutes.

10 GAINING VISIBILITY

Gaining visibility over what your team is doing and what their current results are makes you able to prioritise areas of activity that can be improved so you can make those improvements quickly. It enables you to empower the people in your team so they in turn can deliver in a way that ensures best practice. It also introduces new team members in a way that gets them up and running quickly without reinventing the wheel on what best practice looks like. Finally, it's about publicising your and your team's wins.

Gaining visibility is achieved through a software application that is customised to reinforce the best practice requirements so you get the results you want. It sits in your team's working environment and is accessible through the internet.

How do I gain first-class visibility?

→ **Recognise the importance of gaining visibility.** Start by thinking about what the mission critical activities are within your strategic framework (e.g. innovation, talent management, risk management, project portfolio management). Ask yourself: 'If we are to achieve consistent high performance, is it OK to have an individualised approach to any of these activities? What will happen if we don't get optimal results on these activities and what impact will that have on our goals? If I don't know what the potential roadblocks are on my mission critical projects or how to resolve them, how much will I fall behind on my time to market?'

→ **Understand what you need to monitor, when and why.** Don't monitor everything, but start with your mission critical activities.

→ **Check for consistency with best practice.** Ensure that the information provided enables you to focus on key areas of concern and helps with troubleshooting the root cause.

→ **Finally, think about how the information needs to be presented** – what format, and how the information will be used by different members of the team.

An example

The following screenshot shows a monthly performance report for a City Council. It highlights the key facts from each of the council's improvement initiatives for its current financial year, together with the current Red-Amber-Green status.

Ref.	Title	Description	Owner	Lead Team	% complete	Period	Budget	Project NPV	Start	Close	STATUS	Issues	Stage		
Change Management															
1	ABC Supply chain DEMO	Streamlining electronic ordering using integrated web-based order management system	Bruce (Andy)	Operations	64	2009 - Q2	£10,000	£450,167	13 Mar 2009	7 Aug 2009	1-Red	2	2. Measure		
2	Innovation process	Introduction of cross-business ideas and innovation process	Badeley (George)	Logistics and Supply Chain	54	2009 - Q4	£20,000	£386,167	6 Jan 2009	17 Aug 2009	2-Amber	2	1. Define		
3	Project management infrastructure	The development of org. structure, processes, performance systems and report systems needed to support the delivery of DAL's strategic project portfolio	Project Office(KT)	Service and Support	20	2009 - Q3	£70,000	£339,510	16 Mar 2009	16 Sep 2009	2-Amber		3. Analyse		
							£100,000	£1,175,844	6 Jan 2009	16 Sep 2009	1-Red				
Continuous Improvement															
4	Internal communications	Improvement of internal comms through use of the new intranet	Bruce (Andy)	Logistics and Supply Chain	56	2009 - Q4	£5,000	£145,608	30 Jan 2009	7 Aug 2009	2-Amber	2	3. Analyse		
							£5,000	£145,608	30 Jan 2009	7 Aug 2009	2-Amber				
Information Technology															
5	Cross-functional learning	Database system to capture and transfer operational insights across functions	Welsford (Barry)	Logistics and Supply Chain	60	2009 - Q3	£10,000	£350,167	6 Jan 2009	7 Aug 2009	3-Green	2	5. Control		
							£10,000	£350,167	6 Jan 2009	7 Aug 2009	3-Green				

Engagement, commitment and the line manager

Dr Richard McBain Henley Business School, University of Reading

The line manager plays a key role not only in delivering organisational performance but also in delivering organisational people policies. Recent research has also demonstrated that the line manager plays a vital role in setting the context for the performance of others in the organisation. An employee's experience in their workplace is strongly influenced by their relationship with their line manager, and perceptions of the line manager are emerging as an important factor in developing an individual's attitudes to the organisation and to their job. In turn, these attitudes are linked to important consequences for the organisation and the individual.

One of the most important of these attitudes in the workplace is that of organisational commitment, or the extent to which an individual identifies with and is involved in an organisation.[5] This has been the subject of considerable research and is typically seen as being composed of several elements: affective commitment, or emotional attachment; normative commitment, or loyalty based on obligation; and continuance commitment, based on a recognition of the costs of leaving the organisation.[6] Affective commitment, the most widely researched aspect, is strongly associated with

[5] Mowday, R., Porter, L. and Steers, R. (1982) *Employee-organisation Linkages: The Psychology of Commitment, Absenteeism, and Turnover.* New York, US: Academic Press.

[6] Allen, N. and Meyer, J. (1990) 'The Measurement and Antecedents of Affective, Continuance, and Normative Commitment to the Organisation', *Journal of Occupational and Organisational Psychology* **63**, pp. 1–8.

EXPERT VOICE

job satisfaction, but is distinct from it. A range of factors have been shown to be related to levels of organisational commitment. These include personal factors, such as age and tenure, as well as organisational characteristics, but the most widely researched factors have been the characteristics of the job that an individual performs as well as leadership and line manager behaviours, such as giving feedback and participative decision making.

Organisational commitment matters because higher levels of commitment, and particularly affective commitment, have been linked positively to such outcomes as attendance, individual performance and organisational citizenship. Low levels of affective commitment, on the other hand, are associated with absenteeism and turnover. Given the importance of retaining talent, and the cost of losing it, fostering high levels of organisational commitment could impact on the bottom line for an organisation.

Another key attitude in the workplace that has emerged more recently and has been the subject of widespread practitioner interest in particular is that of employee engagement. There is no single accepted definition, and there is ongoing debate as to whether 'engagement' includes 'commitment' or is a separate attitude. However, engagement, broadly speaking, is 'a positive attitude to the job' and, as with commitment, it has several aspects. An engaged employee is mentally focused on the job, is emotionally involved with it, and puts in the effort and action to achieve the job requirements. Likewise a disengaged employee withdraws mentally, emotionally and behaviourally from the job. There is increasing evidence that engagement matters, for example in terms of customer satisfaction, innovation and financial performance. For the individual, higher levels of engagement seem to be associated with job satisfaction, well-being and individual performance.

As with commitment, there are a number of factors that may promote engagement. These include individual factors such as age and gender, organisational aspects including culture, the leadership of the organisation, aspects of working life such as clarity of purpose, having a meaningful and challenging job, and involvement in decision making, as well as the role of the line manager. Indeed the line manager has often been seen as the key factor in employee engagement, even if the evidence may not always fully support this.

So, what is it that the line manager can do practically to engage and gain the commitment of employees? Although organisational commitment and employee engagement are different things, there are similarities in the sorts of behaviours by line managers that may promote both commitment and engagement. Some of the key behaviours that promote organisational commitment and engagement are:

→ clarity of expectations regarding the job

→ providing opportunities for growth and development

→ providing recognition for an employee's achievements

→ honesty and absence of hidden agendas – words and actions are the same

→ providing employees with access to important people and resources elsewhere in the organisation

→ giving ongoing, constructive, and timely feedback

→ involving others in decisions that impact upon them, and sticking to agreed decisions

→ informing employees about developments in the organisation, which provides the bigger picture and context for the job.

Underpinning these behaviours is a belief that employees should be treated with appreciation and respect, with a genuine concern for their individual interests and well-being. Typically a participative and empowering management style, rather than a controlling or micro-managing one, is more likely to develop positive employee attitudes, although the appropriate style will also depend on the individual employee and their needs. Above all, managers need to be aware of their relationships with their people and develop their trust.

EXPERT VOICE

TECHNOLOGIES

To remain as effective and efficient as possible, Fast Track managers differentiate themselves by the support mechanisms they put in place to help themselves and their team. This includes the intelligent use of appropriate information technologies enabling, for example, the automation of non-core activities and thereby freeing up time to focus on managing, motivating and leading the team. It may also include the use of coaches, peer-to-peer networks and gaining access to the latest thinking in their function.

Getting started

Why consider technology?

There are a number of drivers. The rate of change in the external environment is dramatic. In all industries we see the consolidation of competition, pressures from international markets, emerging new technologies and relentless changes in legislation. How can we possibly keep up and remain aware of what is going on?

CASE STORY *INTERNATIONAL BRAND CONSISTENCY AND SPEED TO MARKET, SARAH'S STORY*

Narrator Sarah is a group marketing manager for an international food and beverage company.

Context An iconic brand in the drinks industry was acquired by a larger entity with a wider distribution network. The company now found itself one of a number of different brand companies in the network.

Issue The big challenge was how to establish the future of the brand platform agenda with consistent input from local markets on brand performance; and also to be able to integrate local market intelligence into a successful long-term strategy for the global brand.

Solution Sarah's solution was to use a web-based tool to provide a series of standard templates and sets of criteria to provide local markets with a consistent framework for reporting on brand performance.

The information is collected quarterly and a report on brand performance generated. This summary is reviewed by the global marketing function. Decisions are then taken as to what the priorities are for the short, medium and longer term.

Learning The company learned that developing competitive advantage depends upon access to local market information, which in turn enables speed to market. It also understood the massive capability of using technology.

There is certainly no shortage of information – frankly, there is too much. How do we sift through the myriad of junk emails, websites, free journals, and mobile texts that arrive uninvited at all times of the day and night?

Whilst information overload is a critical issue, the reality also is that if we don't make use of relevant and up-to-date information we will fall behind the competition. You can make the finest radio receivers in the land but if it is becoming obvious that DAB is taking over and you are not in that technology, you have major problems.

Whilst technology is not the answer to all our problems, it is a very important enabler to help us remain effective and efficient.

 QUICK TIP *LATEST TECHNOLOGIES*
Get someone in the team – they will probably pick themselves – to review the latest technologies once a quarter and look for ways technology could improve the effectiveness of your team.

What activities should we focus on?

Before deciding how to use technology or automation to save time, first eliminate entirely low-value or unnecessary activities.

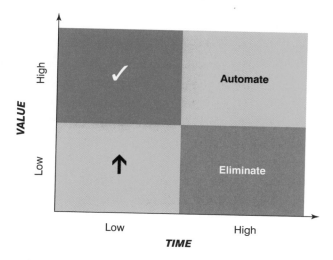

Start by making a map of your current functional and administrative processes, and then make a list of all the current activities across the team. Then assess how much time and resource is spent on each item, and the value you associate with each – perhaps using a simple five-point scale. Then draw a simple two-by-two matrix to assess where each activity falls.

→ Those falling in the bottom right-hand corner are the critical ones to address – high time but low value. Eliminate these. Example: perhaps there are review meetings you don't need to attend or some that could be delegated to a member of your team, which might also be good for their personal development.

→ Those in the bottom left-hand corner pose a problem. They are not consuming much time, so are reasonably efficient, but they are not delivering a lot of value. Perhaps there is a way of improving the value of each activity. You might, for example, change the agenda on a weekly progress meeting to include asking the team to come up with at least one new idea for improvement.

→ Those in the top left box are already efficient and of high value; perhaps they are already automated. Leave them until your next review.

→ There will of course be activities that make a big difference but that take a lot of time to do, such as analysis of the competition or market and customer trends in order to identify breakthrough ideas. These are by definition important and high value (top right-hand corner); so you do not want to get rid of these activities, but you need to find efficient ways of doing them. You may achieve 'Automation' by using technology, such as a web subscription service to send monthly updates on competitors direct to your desktop rather than having to search the internet for new data. Alternatively, it might be as simple as changing the way a regular activity is done to reduce time and effort required, such as using video-conferencing to conduct monthly review and idea generation meetings with distributors.

Think carefully about your overall time management: be aware of how you use your time and constantly look for ways of improving this. Once you have formally conducted this time–value assessment, you will be more conscious of this need. Don't forget that we tend to do those things that we enjoy and put off what is less fun. If you're serious about putting technology to the best possible use, then try to overcome this psychological bias and look at the use of your time as objectively as you can. If you do not manage your time well, you will find it difficult to fit the more strategic tasks in because not doing them doesn't impact your short-term objectives.

When invited to meetings, constantly ask the question 'Why?' What value will the meeting give me, or what value will I give to it? If there is no obvious answer, then decline the invitation or delegate. The key is to remove unnecessary tasks and activities before looking for opportunities to automate: that way you avoid putting IT and other resource into something that has little or no value.

Finally, encourage your team to carry out the same exercise so that when you are deciding on various options for automation you are aiming to increase the overall effectiveness of the team not just yourself.

The process-system link

How should we use information technology?

Think carefully about how you will use technology and ensure it links back to your and the company's strategic framework. Perhaps the starting point is to look at your overall performance management processes and look for opportunities to make each element quicker, simpler and possibly more fun!

Some aspects of the framework will lend themselves to use of technologies, whereas some of the softer areas such as leadership and behavioural change will offer fewer opportunities.

Make sure that the information provided is accurate and timely so that you have the confidence to act on it. Think carefully also about security: who will be using the technology, what information will it contain and how sensitive is the data? Most technologies are becoming more secure but you need to take time to ensure you set them up correctly in the first place, and that you have the appropriate level of security.

Top technologies

How do I know what technology exists?

So now we've agreed the need for technology, systems and automation and where you are going to deploy it for best effect, how do you find out what is available?

Get into the habit of scanning for technology trends on the web, in industry journals or at trade fairs and exhibitions. Look at what other people in your business are reading – particularly those you most admire. Where do they get their information? Take time to understand what technology other firms – perhaps your competitors or suppliers – are using.

But be aware that there is a lot of information available, and there are new technologies coming along all the time. How do you decide what is relevant and what is useful? Start with a healthy scepticism. Investigate the technology, but ask the 'So what' question: is this relevant to my team, and to me; how will it impact performance? As a team leader trying to improve performance, you may want to suggest using new technologies simply to challenge the thinking of others even if it does not impact your own effectiveness or efficiency.

What tools will support a sustainable approach to performance management?

Recognise that the development of technologies is moving so quickly that the list of what is available to you will never be static. Use the following list as a challenge of what is possible, but accept that it is a snapshot of what is happening at a point in time. The key is to get into the habit of constantly scanning this field in search of ideas for improving the effectiveness and efficiency of your strategic framework

QUICK TIP *SEARCH THE INTERNET*
Schedule a monthly half an hour to search the internet for potential sources of ideas and information that could impact performance, and make a list of the top five websites to monitor on a regular basis.

1 The internet – finding potential areas for improvement

What is it?	By now most of us realise that the internet or World Wide Web (www) is a network of interconnected computers where the sharing of information is made possible through use of a common standard called Internet Protocol (IP). This means that we can gain access to information that may be on a computer on the other side of the world so long as we have the necessary access permission. There are two ways of getting information from the web – often referred to as 'push' and 'pull'. Traditionally we go to a website and pull relevant information off as required. However, increasingly we can request to have information 'pushed' at us using streaming technologies. For example, many people now have the latest stock prices or updates on the weather sent to their desktops on a regular basis. Others will get competitive product information when it is announced.
Pros	It provides a rich source of information on a variety of topics. The information is often free and you can get hold of it very fast. The internet can provide a wealth of information about customers and competitors in a matter of minutes where previously it would have taken weeks. It encourages creativity, as noted by US journalist Franklin P. Adams, 'I find that a great part of the information I have was acquired by looking up something and finding something else on the way.' There is also the added benefit of social networking with other like-minded people or communities of practice.
Cons	Most of the information contains a degree of bias. After all someone has produced it for their own purposes. It is also typically unstructured in that a search on a topic will yield lots of results, but the information in each site will be laid out in a different style. Some people call it a repository of several trillion words; the trouble is locating the 25 words you really need.

Success factors	Use the web as a rich source of information and get into the habit of reviewing competitor and customer sites regularly. Beware of information overload, and, if new information is of critical importance, then validate your conclusions using other sources. A neat rule of thumb is the one that journalists use – only publish a 'fact' if you have got at least two reliable sources

2 Electronic suggestion scheme (database)

What is it?	A mechanism by which people throughout the organisation can contribute to a list of new ideas for performance improvement. Intranet technology can make a single list available to everyone.
Pros	It is a quick and easy way of capturing ideas in a single place, and provides an effective way of communicating ideas that one person or team has had to others. This often stimulates new thinking, or the creation of breakthrough concepts that combine several ideas.
Cons	Too many suggestion schemes die a quick death because nothing actually happens to the ideas – typically because of idea overload. If nothing ever seems to happen with these ideas, then people will be discouraged and stop using this mechanism to make suggestions.
Success factors	Use an easily accessible database (ideally on your company intranet) to allow people to capture ideas they may have had, but make sure you restrict the quantity of ideas, and ensure that go/no go/modify decisions are made quickly and communicated back to the originator.

QUICK TIP **HIGH-PERFORMANCE COMPANIES**

Make a list of the best-performing companies you know, and ask what it is that really excites you about them, and what they do differently.

3 Performance improvement and ideas pipeline (database)

What is it?	A team or organisation's ability to meet goals very often depends upon the creation of enough new ideas for products and services to build future revenue streams. Capturing ideas in an 'ideas funnel' ensures that all ideas are evaluated and not lost. Ideas that are seen to have potential can be put through a short feasibility study and then proceed to the next stage in this process. At the next stage ideas would be evaluated for return investment and prioritised. Once an idea has come this far in the process it can be turned into a project.
	Enabling appropriate intervention to bring projects back on track. A series of templates ensure best practice, for example, on project management.
	The suggestion scheme is the process for capturing new ideas and is open to contributions from all stakeholders. In contrast, those more directly involved in performance management tend to use the ideas pipeline. It is a database, or spreadsheet of ideas, that provides a mechanism for screening and prioritising ideas, and enables go/no-go decisions to be made on a structured basis.

Pros	Once the pipeline is made visible to key stakeholders it becomes an effective communication tool. Use of structured fields will dramatically improve the speed and quality of decision making at the regular review meetings. Without a structured and visible approach, the wrong ideas are often selected based on personal bias or level of authority. The person organising the database can quickly detect overlap and competing ideas, and resolve the issue before people waste any time and money.
Cons	If the list is allowed to become too big and cumbersome, it can be seen as too bureaucratic, and it is vital that key stakeholders buy into the filtering criteria.
Success factors	Create a single database of ideas based around a structured screening and prioritisation process, but make sure that it is used at monthly management meetings to drive decision making and kill off bad ideas quickly but sympathetically.
Example	The web-based ideas pipeline below shows all the new process, product and market ideas generated in reviews concerned with performance management. Ideas have been assessed against Business Impact, Risk and Trend in order to set overall priority.

Ref.	Project Title	Description	Project Leader	Stage [Tollgate]	Business Impact	Project Risk	Red Flag	
Channel Marketing								
1	Project A	Full description of the project	Ekroth(Karin)		8	6		
2	Project B	Full description of the project	Bruce(Andy)		4	10		
3	Project C	Full description of the project	Daderman(Lena)		3	6		
Consumer Insight (CISP)								
4	Project D	Full description of the project	Bruce(Andy)		9	4		
Innovation (NPD)								
5	Project E DEMO	To refresh the design of ABC Brand in target market	Daderman(Lena)	Gate 3: Project	8	8		
6	Project F	Full description of the project	Bruce(Andy)		8	8		

4 Performance management software

What is it?	There are software platforms that provide custom-built or ready-made applications for managing strategic frameworks, objectives and KPIs. These can be linked to a dashboard that would feature vision, mission, strategic priorities and goals.
Pros	In this way, individuals and teams take responsibility for recording and measuring their performance through a set of templates that provide standard input criteria. The information is visible to the individuals and team as appropriate so that up-to-the-minute awareness of issues and progress is consistently available and corrective action taken to get back on track.

Cons	Unless thoroughly sold to all the individuals who need to use it and learn from it, such a platform can look complicated and daunting. If there is a high level of resistance at the beginning, it is very difficult to bring people on board later.
Success factors	Make sure that people take it on step by step. If it is a major change for a lot of people, don't forget to do a pilot so that you have a live example to demonstrate as you roll it out to others. Find champions in any area where you are going to implement the platform so that there are local people encouraging new users. People need to see the tool as a simple record of the process and planning work they have already done.

5 Project and portfolio management software

What is it?	Project and portfolio management (PPM) software applications are used to scope, plan, monitor and control the implementation of new ideas using project management techniques. They provide a structured approach to managing a portfolio of complex projects. Most major new performance-oriented initiatives can and should be viewed as projects, and need to be planned as such – too many initiatives fail to deliver against anticipated benefits, often because they are poorly project-managed.
Pros	PPM software provides a very effective way of planning the overall portfolio of project activities, making it clear what the individual priorities are, specific objectives and ultimately who does what and when. Simple outputs can also provide a clear communication mechanism for all stakeholders. Web-based applications used across an organisation provide a means for managing the portfolio of projects as a whole as opposed to managing individual projects in isolation.
Cons	Most project management tools are too complex for performance improvement projects. They tend to focus on detailed task and resource management as opposed to the typical success factors that tend not to be defined – such as having clear objectives, an effective stakeholder management process, and a simple risk register. It is also difficult to accurately forecast the potential future value associated with a new idea, making it difficult to agree specific targets.
Success factors	Be clear about which ideas can be implemented quickly (Just Do It) and which will benefit from project management techniques. Then find a simple and easy to use web-based software product and ensure that key people know how to use it. Finally, don't forget that project and portfolio management is as much about setting the vision and leading the team as plotting the critical path.
Example	The web-based report overleaf shows part of the portfolio of marketing initiatives for a business unit. A simple Red-Amber-Green classification is used to identify projects needing attention. During a review meeting, the team will 'drill down' into the detail of projects needing support.

Ref.	Project Title	Project Leader	Executive Sponsor	Team	Period	Value	Investment	Start Date	Close date	Status	Trend / Red Flag	Buy-in
Market Launch												
1	Market Share [DEMO] Address Q4 shortfall in increased market share target through the introduction of innovative new pricing models	Bruce(Andy)	Edwards (Mark)	Sales and Marketing	09-10 Oct			12 Sep 2008	5 Aug 2009	1-Red		★★★★☆
2	Brand A 2.0 Address Q4 shortfall in increased market share target through the introduction of innovative new pricing models	Martinez-Monroy (Mercedes)	Bruce(Andy)	Sales and Marketing	09-09 Sep			3 Dec 2008	25 Jul 2009	3- Green		★☆☆☆☆
3	Brand B 100 Address Q4 shortfall in increased market share target through the introduction of innovative new pricing models	Prichard(Ryan)	Edwards (Mark)	Sales and Marketing	09-07 Jul			18 Mar 2009	27 Nov 2009	3- Green		★★★★☆
						9,500,000	€340,000	12 Sep 2008	27 Nov 2009	1-Red		
Market Penetration												
4	Global Promotions 1 Address Q4 shortfall in increased market share target through the introduction of innovative new pricing models	Ross(David)	Edwards (Mark)	Sales and Marketing	10-02 Feb			11 Dec 2008	5 Dec 2009	2- Amber		☆☆☆☆☆
5	Portfolio Flavours Address Q4 shortfall in increased market share target through the introduction of innovative new pricing models	Ross(David)	Bruce(Andy)	Sales and Marketing	10-05 May			18 Jan 2009	30 Sep 2009	3- Green		☆☆☆☆☆
6	Pricing Address Q4 shortfall in increased market share target through the introduction of innovative new pricing models	Edwards(Mark)	Edwards (Mark)	Sales and Marketing	10-02 Feb			18 Mar 2009	25 Aug 2009	1-Red		☆☆☆☆☆

6 Talent management systems

What is it?

Talent management systems are built to include:

team development plans

individual development plans, and

an overview of team talents, technical competence and competence frameworks.

The overall aim is to get control of your most important strategic asset – your people.

Pros

The application makes it possible to search for talent for particular roles or projects using the profiling criteria for the role. This means that you can readily match roles between talent and resource mission critical activity quickly and efficiently.

It helps to align organisational roles with the definition of the roles of your people and can cover everything from appraisal to succession planning.

Cons

It is difficult to implement a reliable system of updating the data. If it includes managers' opinions about people as well as facts about their history and skills, you will have to look at access to make sure the wrong information is not getting into the wrong hands.

Success factors

This information is accessible to team leaders across a business in order to plan the use of talented people and 'A' players.

Individual development plans can be recorded and then must be updated. Both the individual and team leader can have access to track progress and next steps. An example of a talent portfolio is shown opposite.

Ref.	Person	Role Description	Stage	Potential	Status	
EMEA						
1	Bruce(Andy) Sales and Marketing Manager [DEMO]	S&M Director for the sale of branded products into European markets	First 100 days	Sales Director	35	▣ ⊡
2	Dunster(Maurice) Operations Director	Operations and Supply Chain Director for regional operations	Performance Management	Level 4	18	▣ ⊡
3	Edwards(Mark) IT Director	Information Systems and Technology Director for EMEA	Performance Management	Level 3	40	▣ ⊡
4	Mackay(Vivienne) Global Talent Director	HR Executive responsible for ensuring the development and utilisation of talent on a global basis	Performance Management	Level 4	85	▣ ⊡
5	Prichard(Ryan) Regional Sales Manager	Sales manager for regional (non core) markets	First 100 days	Level 4	38	▣ ⊡
Global						
6	Martinez-Monroy(Mercedes) External Technical Resource	External Technical resource responsible for the support and maintennce of the SofTools/PU platform	Induction	Level 2	53	▣ ⊡
7	Ross(David) Chief Executive	Cheif Executive for EMEA	Last 100 days	Level 5	68	▣ ⊡
8	White(Cheryl) HR Director	Utilisation and development of global talent	Performance Management	Level 3	88	▣ ⊡

QUICK TIP *GLOBAL PERSPECTIVE*

Take a global view on your local activities and recognise that everything we do is affected by the activities of others, often on the other side of the globe. Talent management systems can cross national boundaries in helping to get the right people into the right roles.

7 Change tracking software – following implementation through

What is it?   Most improvement programmes generate a large number of individual change initiatives, perhaps a hundred or more. A key challenge for the implementation team will be ensuring that these initiatives are fully implemented, and that targets – whether revenue increases or cost savings, are realised and sustainable. This often results in large change programmes failing to deliver sustainable savings to the bottom line.

Pros   Putting a change tracking system in place across the organisation gives visibility and accountability to those responsible for driving change. Using the performance management and project management tools looked at previously means that a change team is in a position to make sure that good ideas are followed through to real implementation – but this only works if it can see what is going on and whether it is on track.

Cons   Unfortunately, resistance to change and the complexity of managing change in large organisations often result in change initiatives not being fully implemented.

Change initiatives often take time to become embedded, resulting in a loss of benefits as organisations revert to past practices after initial implementation.

In both cases a cross-functional team is dependent on 'charismatic power', where their authority comes from their persuasiveness and their results.

Success factors	Get senior people behind this. You need the big battalions on your side. Concentrate on finding a web solution that provides the appropriate levels of visibility and control over change initiatives to all key stakeholders – whether internal or external to the business. Publicise and attribute success and celebrate the achievement of the objectives of the change programme with all the contributors.

8 Social networking software – blogs, wikis and forums

What is it?	These are special websites that allow people to log in and discuss ideas relating to a specific topic in the form of a discussion thread, where the most recent comments are displayed first. Blogs may be created on the internet or on the company intranet, and provide a place where groups of people, internal or external to the organisation, can share ideas.
Pros	It provides a more open form of discussion than emails as the discussion is open for others to see, and is captured for future reference by other teams. Blogs work particularly well where they are focused on a specific topic – sometimes referred to as special interest groups (SIGs), and where they are used to solve specific problems.
Cons	Unless there is a clear reason for going to the blog many people just don't bother, so a team leader has to encourage a team that is working on a particular performance improvement to use it and build it into their normal processes. Blogs often work best for IT teams where they already have a culture of sharing insights and expertise, but sometimes do not work so well with other functions.
Success factors	Consider carefully if you would use a social network and, if so, how? How would you focus it on specific business needs or problems in performance? What would make it exciting and worthwhile enough to make it work within the community, when most people will have other commitments to focus on? Perhaps find a small team that would be interested in piloting a blog on a specific topic, and see how they get on.

9 Digital dashboard

What is it?	A digital dashboard is a term that refers to the presentation of performance data on a computer screen – whether the manager's PC or via an LCD projector in a meeting. The senior member of the team defines the information displayed on a function's or organisation's dashboard. It will contain updates on all performance improvement objectives and change projects.
Pros	If set up correctly, dashboards provide an instant update on progress every time a member of the team logs in to their PC – 'pushing' relevant data directly to the person with the greatest level of interest or need.
Cons	They can be costly to set up, as the underlying data typically needs to be pulled from other databases and put into a format that makes it presentable. Too often the data is not relevant to the individual user, and may not be up to date. Each management level needs a different perspective on the dashboard.
Success factors	Investigate the pros and cons of creating a dashboard for your business – what would it look like, what information would you want to present, and how would it support your strategic framework? Once set up, make sure that it reflects the different needs of the different stakeholders that will be using it.

10 Lessons learned database

What is it?	A central repository of the lessons learned from previous initiatives. It captures basic information about the idea, the initiative leader, and the teams involved. It will ideally also present a 'story' of what was done and why, and what the outcome was (good and bad), and perhaps what the team would do differently next time.
Pros	It is enormously valuable to the business as a means of capturing insights from individuals and teams whilst they remember and before they move jobs – or worse still leave the business. Without active use of a lessons learned database, organisations often repeat mistakes in terms of selecting bad ideas or poor implementation.
Cons	Teams often don't invest the time to stop, think and learn, let alone capture the ideas for future reuse by others. Towards the end of any change project, many members of the team will have moved on to other commitments and they often just don't have the time. Even when insights are captured, people often don't believe that others will bother to look at them, so they are often unstructured and of little value. There is also often a lack of trust in terms of how others will use the information.
Success factors	Make the capturing of insights part of the weekly review meetings with the team, and ensure they are captured and classified in a central and easily accessible database. However, to bring the database to life, make sure that future teams are encouraged to review the database during the initial idea evaluation and project planning phases.

How do I keep balance?

Now stop. Before going out and investing in the latest and greatest, remember that technology is just an enabler. Success will ultimately depend on your ability to lead others, your behaviours and how you interact with others. Be wary of being drawn into new technologies too quickly – let someone else make the mistakes, but then learn quickly. Finally, if you do decide to introduce new systems into your team, think carefully about the possible risks – what could go wrong?

STOP – THINK – ACT
Ask yourself and the team these questions:

What should we do?	What technologies are available that will help to improve performance and create high-performance teams?
Who do we need to involve?	Who would benefit and why?
What resources will we require?	What level of investment would be required?
What is the timing?	When would be a good time to introduce the new technology – is there a 'window of opportunity'?

Visit **www.Fast-Track-Me.com** to capture and track your actions towards high performance.

Managing future performance through an emergent workforce

Nick Horslen Independent business adviser

Those now entering the workforce for the first time are known as 'confident, demanding, materialistic, techno-savvy, carefree and on the move'. Raised by Baby Boomers they appear to be turning Maslow on its head. They come with built-in contradictions and they want, and have, access to so much more. They define their own 'work–life' balance or passion. They expect success and rewards so much more immediately. These young adults are entering the workforce at a time of real change – dramatic change in the economy, in society, and inside organisations.

Change isn't new, but the way that young people now see it has altered. Access to information, the means to collaborate and communicate, the way they see the world and the influences upon them have changed. How they go about daily activities and make plans has changed. None of that change has sprung up instantly overnight; it has been emerging for years, at least a decade, but the new emergent leaders who will be the business leaders for the next 10, 20 or 30 years arrive at their companies, large and small, never having known anything other than their own experience.

From childhood, adolescence and further education, their experience is inseparable from the experience of the internet, Google, Facebook, YouTube, the iPod, sms/txt, skyTV and so on. It's a globally accessible, always on, universally connected world where informal instant relationships complement the longer-term traditional relationships from the past. It is an experience where framing the 'here and now' means constant online communication, constant searching and finding out the things they don't yet know. Through social media, the constant bouncing around of immediate activities, ideas and actions it's an experience that tells them they don't need to sit around and be told or lectured to 'by other people's experts and leaders'. They find out in an instant what they feel to be the right facts, ideas and vision. They blend online and offline conversations and locations into the one real-world, real-time experience, to analyse, entertain and act upon. And while they do this, they can just as easily be sitting on a train, at work, in front of the TV or out enjoying themselves. They bring a new level of multi-tasking which might even suggest their brains get wired differently over time. It's a 24 by 7 paradigm, multimodal, so the idea of boundaries and notions of on and off, in and out has changed.

This next generation know they can see and hear it all as video or sound whenever and wherever they are. They can research trends and verify facts through any wiki, website, validated or invalidated source, all in an instance. They see information and data, they experience sound and vision, they exchange and forward with a new level of linkage across subjects, people, locations and boundaries that previous generations would hesitate over.

With a world that moves at the speed of the internet and tainted with post-9/11 'fear, uncertainty and doubt' (FUD), these new workers have been raised to believe the world is uncertain but there for the taking. With everything at their fingertips, they will take a new view on their own performance, what they need, how they do it and what they are doing it for. After all, experience from the past does not mesh up with the future so they might ask, 'Why is experience relevant?'

Organisations will do well to understand and anticipate this change and what that change means for them and the way things get done. By embracing the emergent nature of that change, those that strike the right accord will bring out the best of the next generation and, by virtue of that approach, build leaders fit for the future.

If these new workers can make the connections so much faster, if they move into a world of connected and 'linked data' then they are poised to see the bigger picture. If they see the flow from data to information to knowledge and wisdom, as they surely will as they grow, then they can act more decisively and faster, putting their needs as individuals before those imposed by traditions, which came with their own embedded group self-interests. In the process, they will create a new playing field whereby leaders are found, sought and followed, and where they are exposed and judged more directly than ever before. The challenges they bring – speed, openness and connectivity – are the very things that will challenge them. Those that thrive and survive will be the leaders of substance for tomorrow. Preparing the ground for that level of performance is a new challenge for today, and who lays the foundation is yet to be identified but it's out there, happening now. Manage the contradictions to gain the best predictions!

Definitions

Baby Boomers (born 1945–61):

→ Defined by post-war optimism

→ Ethos = hard work, loyalty

→ Time-served

→ Status and job titles mattered

Generation X (born 1962–77)

→ End of cold-war certainties

→ Strong political leadership

→ Invented the long-hours culture

→ Digital immigrants

Generation Y (born 1978–98):

→ Natives in a digital world

→ 24/7, anyone, anything, anytime

→ Don't hesitate to question authority

→ Rather than 'seen and not heard' they expect praise, recognition, encouragement and reward – every day!

→ Arrive at work on day one already equipped with the same or better work tools than the ones the workplace provides

→ They assume greater control and accountability over how they work and the impact on the bottom line

→ Will change jobs and career more frequently than any generation before

→ Comfortable with cross-border and cross-cultural changes. 』 』

EXPERT VOICE

5

IMPLEMENTING CHANGE

Having been through the first four chapters of this book, you are probably thinking about how to implement five or possibly six ideas for improvement that you have highlighted in your own mind. This chapter is about helping you to organise your ideas and implement them effectively. The key features are:

→ Prioritisation – which ideas will you implement first?

→ Planning – what is your plan for introducing the change?

→ Dealing with issues – how will you stay on track?

→ Critical success factors – how can we increase our chances of success?

Prioritisation

Let's say you have six ideas you want to introduce. Start by putting them in a prioritised list. To do this, first think about the criteria that you will use to evaluate your ideas. Here are some you can use to evaluate the options and then decide on your priorities list:

→ Does this idea have an impact on your mission and **goals** in the short, medium or longer term? If it does not, then it's not a high priority – it's a nice to have.

→ Is it easy or not so **easy** to make this change?

→ What is the **return on investment (RoI)** going to be from making this change? Is it worth the time, energy and financial cost? Does this have an impact on our goals?

→ Do we have the **resources** required to make this change? Financial, material or other.

→ Do we have the **people** necessary to support making the change? What is our capability and capacity to make this change?

→ What favourable impact will this change have on **stakeholders**? Does anyone else need to agree with this change outside your team? Your peer group, boss or other functions may have experience that would deter or encourage you to make this change.

See how this works in the simple example below. Imagine that you have identified the following aspects of your performance management framework that you and your team feel represent the greatest opportunities for improvement:

→ **Idea 1:** Engage the team in developing a new strategic framework.

→ **Idea 2:** Establish a clear set of KPIs for delivering against the framework.

→ **Idea 3:** Do a high-performance team gap analysis and agree an action plan with the team to close that gap.

→ **Idea 4:** Evaluate team members to determine your 'A' players.

→ **Idea 5:** As an example we can follow, let's take a specific idea for change. Work with the team to develop a core culture that defines how the organisation will treat its key accounts.

Each of the ideas has been evaluated using a five-point scale where 5 represents a strong and beneficial impact on the criterion and 1 represents a poor impact.

CRITERION	IDEA 1	IDEA 2	IDEA 3	IDEA 4	IDEA 5
Link to goals	5	3	3	2	4
Easy to implement	4	4	3	1	5
Value/RoI	5	4	5	2	4
Resources	2	5	4	3	4
People	4	4	4	2	5
Stakeholders	5	3	4	2	5
Totals	25	23	23	12	28
Priority	2	3	4	No go	1

The overall score provides a basis on which to set priority, but the performance against each criterion will also identify areas where you will need to focus during implementation of the change. Idea 1, for example, is a strong idea, but to implement the change successfully you will need to address the issue of lack of resources. Also, be prepared to reject ideas that you initially thought were good. Idea 4, for example, should be rejected because it will either prove impossible to implement, or not result in real and significant improvement in performance that has a useful impact on shareholders.

 QUICK TIP ASK 'WHY?'
To generate new ideas for improvement, get into the habit of asking 'Why?'. Why do we produce this product or service in the way we do? Why do we approach customers in the way we do? and so on.

Planning

So you've got great ideas for improvement, but how do you start to implement them? Clearly these changes are significant and it would therefore be unwise to just do it, but at the same time you need to get on and these ideas might provide an opportunity to make an impression. It is vital that implementing these changes goes well.

You are now ready to make a start on **Idea 5** – your top performer. Recognise that there is no one right approach to creating a sustainable approach to improving the performance of your team, but you will need to think ahead about your own particular situation and plan the changes carefully. Here is a checklist of things to consider when planning your changes:

1 State the outcome: 'What specifically is this change you want to implement and what is its purpose?' We want to create a new way of approaching our key customers to increase the volume and profitability of sales to them and at the same time locking them in more firmly to dealing with us.

2 Describe the present situation before implementing the change. All customers are treated the same in terms of discounts, marketing communication, sales effort and local support.

3 Describe what successful implementation will look like, feel like and sound like to yourself and others. What are the benefits? What are the opportunities and risks? After implementing some sort of key account management programme, we will have national control of the accounts and a consistent approach to all their divisions and subsidiary companies. The benefits are improved volume and profitability of sales to these customers. We will achieve a relationship more akin to a partnership with the key accounts with much higher levels of contact. The major risks are that we annoy all the other customers who could feel discriminated against and that the key accounts feel more powerful in dealing with us and thus able to demand better delivery terms and discounts.

4 What is the first step and the order and sequence of events required to successfully implement this change? Joint planning sessions with marketing and sales followed by an investigation into best practice in this area and a search for other people's experience in this area.

5 What resources do you need?

> → Implementation team – a small joint marketing and sales team for the investigative work and a review committee that sits from time to time.
> → Financial – we need a rough budget of £15,000 for expenses and the buying in of information and expertise.
> → Stakeholder support.

6 Who are the individuals on the team that you need to execute the plan? What are the implications for current workload and priorities? There are two key people we need to second on to the project: one from marketing and a first or second line sales manager. The release of both will damage their functions unless we take mitigating action.

7 What is the deadline for completion? Depending on the RoI of the project we will aim to have a full proposal for the board in six months.

8 What will you gain from this change? A more profitable and professional approach to our markets and a stepping stone for rolling the approach out to our international operations.

9 What will you lose? If we don't get it right we could lose the goodwill of non-key customers. We will have to handle the position of the sales teams working with local divisions of the key accounts. We need their help and must not demotivate them.

 CASE STORY COMPLEX PRODUCT KEY ACCOUNTS, ERIC'S STORY

Narrator Eric was the account manager for a large aerospace manufacturer selling complex electronic instruments.

Context Being in aerospace, a customer constantly pushed Eric's products to their limits. Eric's company had to bring out new ways of doing things frequently and this customer was always a leading implementer.

Issue Eric had to coordinate and motivate a number of departments – marketing, research and development and production, to name the top three – in response to this difficult but very important customer's needs. At times he needed director level support but could lose time in escalating the issue and getting a mandate to solve it.

Solution Eric influenced the account management implementation team to gain agreement to the appointment of a senior executive as a 'sponsor' of every key account. Eric could then keep that sponsor involved with the customer itself and aware of both his plans and those of his customer. This meant that Eric could get much quicker reaction to escalated problems. The sponsor also had direct knowledge of where the key accounts were heading.

Learning Make sure you listen and react to line management when you are on the staff side of implementing a change project. Be prepared to change your strategy to meet customer needs.

Making a plan

Once you have the objectives you're in a position to make a list of the activities involved in achieving them. Take time to identify ownership, timing and resource requirements, asking what is necessary for success.

Idea 5: Create a core culture that defines how the organisation will treat its key accounts

Phase 1: Select the key accounts

Activity 1.1: Design a simple template for analysing customer profiles, and set up an electronic template on the intranet for sales-people globally to apply for their accounts to be included.

Activity 1.2: Make people aware of the new site, and hold a series of competitions to encourage people to get the thing off the ground by submitting ideas, making it as clear as you can at this stage what the selection process will be.

Activity 1.3: Select the accounts that best meet the criteria and com-municate the results to all key stakeholders – taking time to visibly reward the best applications.

Phase 2: Customer access

Activity 2.1: Investigate the feasibility of allowing key account customers to access a limited part of the intranet to give them speedy information on, for example, support issues, product changes and delivery dates.

Activity 2.2: Conduct a pilot with a few customers and, if successful, quickly roll out the approach.

At the end of each phase of your implementation, stop and formally assess performance. These review points are called milestones, where you check that you have achieved what you set out to achieve. Now look at a timeline and produce a Gantt chart showing what is to be done and by when. An example is shown below.

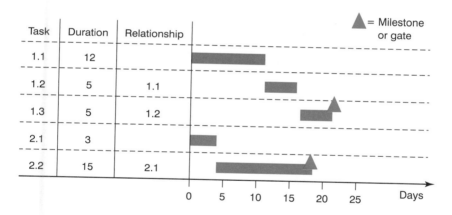

Task	Duration	Relationship
1.1	12	
1.2	5	1.1
1.3	5	1.2
2.1	3	
2.2	15	2.1

▲ = Milestone or gate

0 5 10 15 20 25   Days

It may be that the other elements of your performance management framework can be implemented with informal meetings with the management team and specialists within market research. Remember, an implementation plan can be very useful, but some activities are straightforward enough not to need one.

So, coming away from the specific example of key account management and back to the performance management change, you now have an outline plan of how to implement a series of change projects to reach a company-wide (or division-wide or just for your team) performance management framework. The time has come to get everyone to buy in to it by communicating it to all the stakeholders. Avoid surprises wherever possible so involve key people early in the planning process. You can do this with a conference or a series of emails. You probably also need a newsletter, but recognise that it takes time and skill to get it right. Don't publish too many newsletters or you'll start to find that there is nothing this month really to report. Eventually you'll find that providing a flow of information about the framework will be one of the most important roles managers have.

Produce a report that summarises what needs to be done to set the organisation up optimally. Your report must include some risk analysis, pointing out not only what has gone wrong in the past but also what has worked.

> **QUICK TIP ADVERTISE YOUR CHANGES/ SUCCESSES**
> Don't forget to advertise your successes. Your website, for example, should include enough information about performance improvement to get people curious.

You'll need budget and resources beyond the individual projects. Work out what ideally you will need, remembering that you will have to justify the expense and resources. It's probably not sufficient to say that without improvement the organisation will die. You need more specifics and you need to relate the proposed idea to the achievement of business goals. Look for success stories of companies who have done it before. Point to things that have gone wrong in the past and how much they have cost the organisation. Look for quick wins – simple things you can do before you get your new budget or things that you can implement quickly afterwards. Make the quick wins as concrete in financial terms as you possibly can.

Dealing with issues

Maintain a weekly issues log and bring these to the implementation team once a week to discuss and resolve. Don't forget to log the actions and results.

Now you have to keep project plans on track. Simply putting a plan together does not mean it will happen. Think about the three Ps that you will need to manage – plan (tasks and timings), people (keeping stakeholders motivated and on track) and performance (the project objectives) – and keep your attention balanced between all three.

The PDCA cycle – see the figure below – is a continuous improvement approach to managing a project or team. Use it as a structured approach to monitoring performance and progress, and for remaining alert to the unexpected:

→ **Plan** your activities – you will have done this already if you have a Gantt chart like the one above.

→ **Do** implies completing the activities necessary for success.

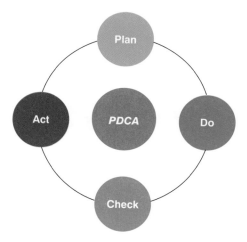

→ **Check** the progress you're making towards implementing the plan. This will reveal any problems in any of the three areas concerned. Here are some examples of what will emerge in the electronic suggestions scheme of phase 1. Plan: a resource that you need will not be available at the time you had planned to have it. Can you change the plan so that the overall timescale is not affected? People: a person you are relying on is getting the tasks done but taking much longer than was expected. Do you change the plan or bring in someone else to speed things up? Performance: the pilot scheme is producing financial benefits but not as much as had been planned. Do you cut costs or search for a way of improving performance?

→ **Act** – make decisions that will bring the project back on track by resolving the problems.

> **QUICK TIP** *ASK 'SO WHAT?'*
> Look for ideas in all areas of performance improvement. For example, if you find a new course on succession planning ask yourself, 'So what will that expenditure of people and money do for us?'

What routines should we set up?

Complex situations can be dramatically simplified through regular structured review meetings. Depending on what you are looking to achieve, these may be quick and simple five-minute updates in the coffee room, or more in-depth, one-day workshops involving all key stakeholders. Reflect on all of your regular meetings:

→ daily, weekly, monthly – focus on performance monitoring and issue resolution

→ annual cycles – focus on strategic planning and priority setting.

How do we stay flexible?

Whilst you need to understand the principles of planning, and performance monitoring, you also need to stay flexible and responsive to the team, be aware of how things are going and changes in the external environment. Think about how tight or loose your controls really need to be. Too loose and you run the risk of missing deadlines and going off at a tangent, but too tight and you run the risk of reducing the team's motivation and losing key stakeholders' commitment.

Nowhere is this tight versus loose leadership style more visible than when a team leader or change project manager uses some of the tools and techniques of project management and gets bogged down by them. Take the example of critical path analysis: this is a useful tech-nique that shows the leader and the team what activities are critical to the completion of the plan on time. You can afford other activities, ones not on the critical path, to slip a bit without compromising the end date of the plan. It's a useful guide for both planning the timing of activities and monitoring progress. But don't get too carried away with it or you risk damping down the creativity of the team and causing motivational problems by an unhealthy concentration on the tasks as you planned them. Critical path analysis can be helpful but, in the end, it's the people not the tight process that will deliver the results you want. There have been situations where the project manager was so intent on ticking off the activities on the project network that people were ignoring shortcuts and better ways of doing things just to keep him happy.

QUICK TIP *DAY-TO-DAY ACTIVITIES*
Look for ways to build creative thinking into day-to-day activities.

Balance the team's rational thinking with tapping into their creative tal-ents. Encourage innovation in performance management even while you're involved in setting up such an environment. You will spot the people who will help more on one side of the rational/creative spectrum, and learn to rely on the rational ones to keep the project steady and the creative ones to make a huge step forward from time to time. Some people go from one mountain top to the next one by plodding down the mountainside then plodding up the other one. Others prefer to take a run and a leap and hope they make it. When they do, they have made a great contribution to the team; when they fail, you and the team will have to help them recover. It's the balance of the two that ensures not only success but also the best result possible.

Critical success factors

As you start to implement ways of improving performance, reflect on the factors that will drive success. You can't focus on everything at once, so where do you start?

Whilst your first approach may be comprehensive, it should not necessarily be difficult to implement. However, there will be barriers, and success appears to come down to getting the following factors right:

→ Focus on opportunities of high value that fit with current business priorities. This tends to get everyone's attention and commitment.

→ Ensure that the senior team shows *active* commitment to the processes you are implementing: after all they will have the greatest impact on business culture, and if they don't take them seriously then no one else will.

→ Get a balanced team in terms of skills, experience and behaviours, if possible, and ensure sufficient budget and resources are allocated to the overall implementation process.

→ Build continuous improvement techniques into business-as-usual in order to minimise the perceived workload or overhead associated with such activity. This is best done through lots of small changes such as modifying a meetings agenda, or adding an item to a weekly checklist.

→ Install systems and tools to support the consistent application of best practices across all teams – effectively creating a 'common performance management language'.

→ Develop skills to improve the quality of the work people do in idea generation and project management as this will improve the overall effectiveness and efficiency of the process.

→ Reward people for sharing ideas and knowledge, in non-financial ways as well as through bonuses.

→ Evaluate progress and performance honestly, openly and without politics, making sure that evidence supports your conclusions and that it is presented in a blame-free way.

→ Finally communicate successes or 'quick wins' to all interested stakeholders so that people can see that the overall approach is working and worthwhile.

The people thing

In the end the performance you are trying to influence involves getting people on board and willing to change their behaviour. That's why implementing change is such an important skill for managers to learn and perfect. Managing change can be a depressing business but there is hope in one simple rule. If you have to manage a change process, you need 'agents of change' to support you. Agents of change are people who fundamentally agree with the need for change and have the will to go through the process themselves.

What I have found in practice is that if 20 per cent of the people involved in the change will act as your agents of change, then your chances of success are good. Less than 10 per cent and you may have to drop your aspirations a bit until you have got more support.

To a large degree change management, for that is what this really is, is about overcoming resistance and people's fears and objections to your plan. You have to be well prepared when implementing changes in a business as not everyone will think like you. You have to deal with people's resistance to change, not try to prevent it.

To that end many successful managers have adopted the DREC curve as a means of understanding people's attitudes to your changes – this is covered in more detail in Chapter 7, Leading the team. DREC stands for the four 'emotions' you may come across whilst introducing a new financial management framework: for example, denial, resistance, exploration and commitment. You will see in Chapter 7 that the phrases seek to illustrate reactions to an event, but what is important is the curve through the four quadrants. How you manage these reactions is crucial to the smooth implementation of change.

STOP – THINK – ACT

Now at the end of this chapter, you will be aware that implementing a comprehensive approach to performance management is not necessarily quick or easy. It needs to be planned and implemented using a disciplined approach. Use the team audit in Chapter 2 to identify the gaps in your current approach to it. (Note that there is a more comprehensive team audit in the Director's Toolkit in Part D.) Then identify the actions you will need to take to make it succeed.

What should we do?	What stages and tasks are appropriate?
Who do we need to involve?	Who needs to be involved and why?
What resources will we require?	What information, facilities, materials, equipment of budget will be required?
What is the timing?	How long will each activity typically take?

Visit **www.Fast-Track-Me.com** to use the Fast Track online planning tool.

EXPERT VOICE

Managing marketing performance

Professor Roger Palmer Henley Business School, University of Reading

Marketers occupy a unique position in the spectrum of management skills; they have primary responsibility for revenue generation, but have little direct authority to implement change. Yet change is their stock in trade and reason for existence. To be effective, marketers need not just functional skills but also the ability to align and coordinate the activities of the firm. Marketers increasingly need, in addition to their functional skills, a high level of managerial capability. Marketing then has a highly strategic role to play and is critical to achieving sustainable competitive advantage.

In an increasingly competitive environment this requires a shift in thinking. Axiomatically, in the business world we view our marketplace through the lens of 'product' (or a service which is invariably productised). Hence we almost unquestioningly think about the success of our business in terms of product profitability and longer-term measures such as market share. In fact most organisations can demonstrate exhaustive analysis of product cost and profitability, yet fail to understand even the most basic metrics relating not to products but to customers. In today's largely mature markets populated by sophisticated and indeed aggressive buyers, achieving competitive advantage by developing 'better' products is increasingly difficult; most products are the same these days.

Marketing success will increasingly depend upon much more insight and understanding, not just of what customers want, but also of what they value. Organisations will need to be flexible and dynamic in order to respond to customers' requirements for lower prices and higher value and this has significant implications for companies. Leading companies truly understand their customers' businesses to the extent that they can proactively offer value opportunities which they can then satisfy. Rolls-Royce Aero Engines not just offers some of the best and most highly engineered products in the world, but also understands that its airline partners don't actually want engines, they want the power the engines provide. Rolls-Royce therefore offer their TotalCare® solution and airline partners pay only for the time in which the engine is operating, with the supplier taking responsibility for spares, maintenance, breakdowns, etc.[1]

Value-based solutions such as this mean that companies must significantly reconfigure their processes, invest in their customers and identify best in class suppliers working with them, by developing cooperative, value creation networks in which all members create and deliver value for the end user.

Yet how many companies can envisage this brave new world? There are very few companies that truly understand not product but *customer* profitability. The cost of manufacturing a product or delivering a service is often known in detail, yet the cost of gaining a customer, the rate of customer turnover or 'churn', and the net profitability of that customer, is largely unknown. Some companies are leading exponents of this understanding of customer economics (e.g. mobile phone operators) and regularly measure their strategy in terms of customer churn, ARPU (average revenue per user) and other key customer-based metrics. However, such metrics represent the underlying strategy of the firm, built around customers and an understanding of their value to the firm, and vice versa.

Marketing strategy based around deep insight and understanding of customer value requirements, delivered through flexible processes and dynamic networks and measured by different, relevant and customer-based metrics represents a significant opportunity – and challenge – for many firms and organisations.

[1] http://www.rolls-toyce.com/civil/services/totalcare/

CAREER
FAST TRACK

Whatever you have decided to do in terms of developing your career as a manager, to be successful you need to take control, plan ahead and focus on the things that will really make a difference. You need to ask yourself how you get into your company's key talent pool.

The first ten weeks of a new role will be critical. Get them right and you will be off to a flying start and will probably succeed. Get them wrong and you will come under pressure and even risk being moved on rather quickly. Plan this initial period to make sure you are not overwhelmed by the inevitable mass of detail that will assail you on arrival. Make sure that other people's priorities do not put you off the course that you have set yourself.

Once you have successfully eased yourself into your new role and gained the trust of your boss and the team, you can start to make things happen. First, focus on your leadership style and how it needs to change to suit the new role; then focus on the team. Are they the right people and, if so, what will make them work more effectively as a project team?

Finally, at the appropriate time, you need to think about your next career move, and whether you are interested in getting to the top and becoming a company director. This is not for everyone, as the commitment, time and associated stress can be offputting, but the sense of responsibility and leadership can be enormously rewarding.

You've concentrated on performance up until now – now it's time to look at your Fast Track career.

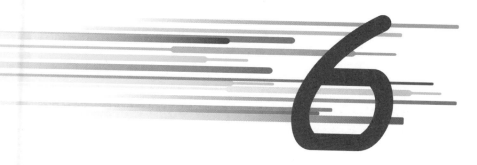

THE FIRST TEN WEEKS

The 'first ten weeks' of starting a new role as the leader of any team are probably the most critical – get them wrong and you risk failure, get them right and you will enjoy and thrive in your new role. What do you need to do, where should you focus, and what must you avoid at all costs?

To enable the new leader to take control, the Fast Track manager will seek to understand key facts, build relationships and develop simple mechanisms for monitoring and control – establishing simple but effective team processes. Again, this task will be simplified using modern technologies and so become effortless and part of day-to-day behaviour.

Changing roles

Why is this a critical time?

It's vital to gain sufficient traction during the first 10–12 weeks in a new role. In big organisations the 'mortality' rate for people in new roles is high at 15–25 per cent. The reason for this is that human beings are set up to operate with a habitual set of behaviours for success. These 'ways of being' are established in a particular context where there is a specific culture, different goals and expectations. When the context changes we attempt to reuse our old strategies for success and very often find that they don't produce the results that we were expecting. There then follows a period where we try to adapt to find new approaches and switch to different behaviours. As we take that action, the environment we are working in is moving on at a pace and we are left trying to catch up.

Whenever you start a new role or job, whether within your existing business or joining a new company, you have an opportunity to make a positive impression on others. However, recognise that you will only get one chance to make a first impression[1] – get the first few months wrong and it could impact your relationships with others for a very long time.

During a period of transition, the team you will be joining will have few preconceptions. People will typically have an open mind and be willing to try new ideas, giving you the benefit of the doubt. We often see this phenomenon when consultants are called in to resolve a critical business issue. They often say exactly the same things as some of the internal managers, but as outsiders their views are respected and acted upon.

This is typically a period of high emotional energy, and activities will often get a higher level of enthusiasm and commitment. Use this time wisely and you will gain significant advantage.

Make sure that you let go of all associations with your old role so that you can focus on your new role. Prepare yourself mentally for the next role by seeing yourself there. This will ensure that you project yourself as being capable and motivated to keep on promoting your career. Promote your team's successes; let people know about the team's achievements and what they are capable of delivering.

What are the potential pitfalls?

Whilst this period of transition presents opportunities to make a good impression, take care not to get it wrong. Few people recover from a bad start in a new role. You will be faced with a number of challenges to overcome:

→ You will need to accelerate learning since you will lack knowledge and expertise in your new role. This will make you vulnerable to getting decisions wrong.

→ In every team there will be a mixture of people and politics. Getting in with the wrong people or setting up favourites can limit your opportunities for future promotion.

[1] Watkins, M. (2003) *The First 90 Days*, Boston MA: Harvard Business School Press.

→ There will be a lot to do in a short period of time, and you may well feel overwhelmed by it all.

→ Most effective managers rely heavily on their informal networks, but in the early stages of a new job these don't exist.

What is the worst-case scenario?

Because people often give the benefit of the doubt to those who are starting a new job or joining a new team, things often go well for a period of time. If you make mistakes they will forgive you because you're new to the job. This is referred to as the 'honeymoon period'. New football coaches, for example, are allowed to lose the first few games without too much criticism. However, after a period of time (the first ten weeks), you, like the coaches, will need to perform well, meeting the expectations of key stakeholders and winning.

During this initial period, it is vital that you take the steps necessary to set yourself up for longer-term success, or else run the risk of, as it were, falling into the chasm[2] (see the figure below). You make a good start but then people start to see the changes you are proposing as just another management initiative. Plan your first ten weeks carefully in order to set yourself up for longer-term success.

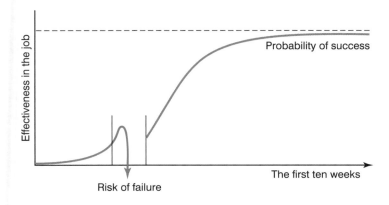

[2] Adaptation of concepts presented in Moore, G. A. (1999) *Crossing the Chasm*, Harper Business.

The first ten weeks

What should I do before I start?

Before starting a new project or job within the area of innovation, you need to do your research in terms of what it will entail and what some of the potential problems are likely to be. Develop a personal to-do list of things to get ready or put in place.

QUICK TIP *TEN MINUTES OUT*
Get into the habit of taking ten minutes out each day simply to browse the internet and search for experiences and benchmarks that are useful in improving performance.

Think also about how you yourself will need to change. How will you behave differently, what knowledge will you need to gain and what new skills would be useful? Understanding these things will help to build your confidence.

If possible, it would also be useful to identify key influencers in your particular function, such as industry experts or your internal experts, and start to build your reputation through your involvement in events or discussion forums.

What do the first ten weeks look like?

Use the following suggestions to put together a plan for your first ten weeks in your new position. Whilst you will get into the detail of each area in your first ten weeks, recognise that you may be able to make a start before you take the job or start in your new role.

Week 1: Get to know your stakeholders

First impressions will influence the way a relationship will develop in the first few months. Obtain organisational charts and start by understanding the stakeholders who are key to you and your team. These will typically include: your boss, work colleagues, your team, functional heads, key opinion leaders, subject matter experts, customers and suppliers.

Do not go into initial meetings or telephone conversations without stopping and thinking them through. What is the impression you want to give, and what do you need to do to make sure this will happen. Think about what could go wrong, and what you can do to make sure risks are avoided or mitigated. Make sure that initial conversations focus on them not you, so take time to really understand what their agenda is, what their concerns are and what their ideas are for the future. Remember how important it is to understand each individual's motivation, strengths and weaknesses. Try not to state your ideas at the initial meeting – it is much better just to listen hard. Indeed it is often said that influence most belongs to the person who says least during the meeting but provides the summary at the end and proposes the action plan. After all, these are the first of regular meetings that you will hold subsequently as you find out, particularly with your direct reports, how they think and how they impact current performance. Find out what stakeholders think needs to change in order to meet goals and create the future.

Find out from senior people the culture that they are trying to build and make your first estimate of who are the main influencers in the business.

It is worthwhile assessing each stakeholder group on a power vs support matrix (see the figure below). Focus on those stakeholders who have the greatest power or influence over your work, and try to understand the politics of the situation. Think hard about how you can win round highly influential people that will oppose your ideas (top left), and consider ways of using the support of your advocates to win round other opinion leaders (top right).

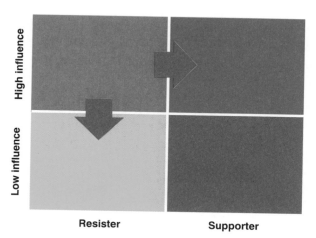

Develop a communication plan that includes face-to-face discussions where possible to improve the support for your team from all the highly influential stakeholders. Finally do not overlook the fact that a key stakeholder may well be the previous incumbent of the job you are starting; if they are still around and available, take time to learn from their previous successes and failures.

Give yourself a stretching objective for these meetings – try and be able to understand the current strategy or plan the team is working on and contrast that plan with the current situation. Align the plan to the overall plan for the company and resolve to update, reframe or refresh it in the coming weeks.

Week 2: Capture a business snapshot

You obviously need to understand the business you are working in, but this should go beyond a superficial knowledge of its products and markets. Get to know that the priorities are, and the critical success factors for this current year.

Everyone should understand the basis on which the company competes, but this is particularly critical for performance management, as all new ideas for performance improvement should be linked in some way to the business's unique selling proposition.

Assess the current state of the business. Is it a new or start-up business, a steady state organisation in a mature market, in the process of rapid growth, a business turnaround in order to regain profitability, or possibly even in a wind-down phase? The current health of the business will guide the focus of your new ideas.

Your quick snapshot should also confirm what budgets and resources you have to achieve your aims and how it has changed from previous years. Use the checklist in the next section to confirm that you have the information you need.

QUICK TIP *STOP NON-VALUE-ADDED ACTIVITIES*
Look to find ways of stopping individual and team activities that don't add value in order to free up time for everyone to stop and think creatively.

Week 3: Create a team SWOT

You know enough now to critically evaluate each aspect of your team and identify those areas that you consider to be strengths and weaknesses, and areas that reflect opportunities and threats. Make a quick list, but then prioritise it down to the top five in each category. Perhaps use the team audit checklist in the Director's Toolkit (p. 180) to add structure to your analysis, and then summarise your thoughts in the form of a SWOT analysis.

Recognise that this will reflect your first impressions, so some of your conclusions will be valid whilst others may be incorrect. Take time to validate your thoughts with your boss and other key stakeholders, this will provide an opportunity to get to know them better and to start thinking about ways to address weaknesses and exploit strengths. Here's an example from a marketing perspective:

Strengths	Weaknesses
CEO enthusiasm for marketing	No common marketing strategies across functional teams, making the central efforts inefficient and ineffective
Clear marketing objective for the current year	
	Limited visibility of current initiatives
Committed marketing team with sufficient budget and time	Poor learning at end of projects
Opportunities	**Threats**
Key account programme could be driven by this central team	Poor reputation of central marketing could lead to reduction in budget
Key account management programme needs to be redesigned	

This marketing manager has identified weaknesses in the way initiatives are managed across the business and the level of visibility the overall marketing programme has at the senior management team level. At the same time, he/she believes that they have a great team and the full support of the senior manager.

QUICK TIP LOOK FOR EVIDENCE

Analyse the facts and opinions of others in order to get to the facts – seek concrete examples. Making decisions on poor information will lead to poor plans.

Week 4: Secure quick wins

It's important for your boss, peer group and direct reports to feel confident in your appointment to this role. From the opportunities analysis you did in week 3, decide on opportunities that will deliver quick wins and that demonstrate your grip on the situation.

Accept that you will not be able to fix everything all at once, but by week 4, people will be watching closely to see what you are actually going to do to make a difference. Make a list of your ideas for change as you progress during week 3, and then prioritise them in terms of impact on the business and urgency. Measure impact in terms of how each change will support a specific business imperative, or the difference it will make to overall profitability. Measure urgency in terms of specific deadlines that need to be met or windows of opportunity, such as implementing a process change during the summer holiday period.

Then for those changes that you consider to be a priority, identify one or two that you know you can implement quickly, within a few days, and with little risk. These are referred to as 'early wins' and, so long as they are not viewed as trivial, will do a lot to boost your credibility within the organisation assuming they succeed.

 CASE STORY *GETTING A QUICK WIN, GRAHAM'S STORY*

Narrator Graham was regional manager of a large telecommunications company.

Context Graham joined to help senior management to implement a huge change programme aimed at knocking the old-fashioned corners off those managers who had served with the organisation since time immemorial.

Issue Many of these managers were accustomed to a hierarchical, rather deferential culture where seniority counted highly. They were also struggling with the concept that the customer was king.

Solution On his very first day the new boy took action on this, using the car park as his vehicle. He removed every car parking space allocated on the basis of management seniority. He reallocated the best spaces to customers only. Also in his tour of the car park he realised that there were some areas that were not only dark but also outside the range of the security cameras. Accordingly, he allocated the next best spaces nearest to the entrance to those women who sometimes or regularly worked late. At a stroke he got the support of those of his people who felt held back by the old guard, and of the more ambitious women willing to work long hours. The old guard was furious and wrote emails complaining to any senior manager they could think of.

Once it became clear that Graham's strategy would prevail, some of the old guard took the redundancy packages that were on offer at the time. The rest followed at times to suit their personal situations.

Learning Do something quickly that is obviously a sensible decision, pleasing the people who are important to the business even if it means cutting across the sensibilities of others who are resisting change. Something that stirs things up at an early stage is not necessarily a high-risk strategy.

Think carefully about potential problems and take time to meet with the relevant stakeholders to ensure fast success. You can then communicate these quick wins in a way that builds commitment to your approach to performance management and its credibility.

In the marketing example in the section above, an effective quick win might be to conduct a one-day workshop with the different sales teams across the business, and simply capture and share their respective new ideas and problems. During the workshop ask each team participant to present their approach to assisting marketing, and then facilitate a discussion about the benefits of creating a common approach. If successful, you will not only have built credibility amongst a key group of people, but you will have started the process of creating common practices and increasing visibility of the overall marketing portfolio. Use this as an opportunity to create a learning culture, and to show that you are open to good ideas from all the teams.

Week 5: Create a vision

At the end of your first month in your new role, stop and take stock of where you are. Reflect on what you have learnt, and the key messages you have received from your boss and other key stakeholders. You should now have enough information and insights to put together your vision for the team for the next two to three years.

Start at the end by thinking about what you want to have achieved before you move on to your next role, whether it be in six months or three years. The clearer your vision of what success will look like, the more likely it is that you will achieve it. Think about how you want people to remember you after you have moved on: what will they say about you?

Then translate this vision into a team strategy or plan. This should clarify what you will do in terms of the products and services you provide and perhaps, just as importantly, what you're not going to do. Clarifying boundaries helps to focus the team and ensure that your limited innovation resources and budget are not spread too thin. Then think carefully about who your customers are, whether internal or external to the business, and which are the most important.

Your vision should also clearly articulate your approach to each of the Fast Track top ten elements in Chapter 3, what you see as the biggest gaps and how and when each will be closed. At this stage it does not need to be detailed, but it should provide a road map stating clearly what you are looking to achieve. You will of course need to take time to validate your plan with members of the team and with your boss. Finish the vision by establishing clear individual and team expectations and performance measures. Make sure that all your stakeholders are aligned to the goals for your team, then set about aligning your team through creating a clear strategic framework.

As well as putting a plan in place for the team, think about the capabilities you personally need to build in order to successfully lead the team. Where there are gaps, create a personal development plan (PDP) for gaining the necessary skills or experience.

Don't forget that these are the first versions of all your plans and activities list. They will alter and become more certain as time passes and your and the team's knowledge expands.

Finally, at this stage you should reflect on the new role and ensure that you are able to balance your work commitments to your preferred lifestyle (and encourage team members to do the same). There is no point in doing a great job if you burn out in the next ten months!

Week 6: Take a break!

By the end of week 5 you will hopefully have done a great job, but you will also be pretty tired. Even the most capable and confident managers tend to use up a lot of nervous energy when getting stuck in to a new job. Try to remain calm and avoid getting stressed.

Use this week to take time to relax and get to know the team better. Whilst you will already have got to know your team in week 1, spend more time with each of them on a one-on-one basis and listen to their views, their aspirations and their concerns.

Establish early on who your 'A' players are. Set about planning to remove low performers and replace them with the right calibre of person, using your competency framework and talent framework. Seek help from your boss and peer group to identify capable talent elsewhere in the business that you could bring in quickly.

Talk to each of your key stakeholders again, and test the various elements of your vision, updating it as you go.

> **QUICK TIP** *REVIEW MEETINGS*
> Get into the habit of asking your team to identify one idea for improvement at the end of each of your regular team meetings.

Pay particular attention to your boss, and get to understand them better. What is their preferred leadership style, what are their major opportunities and threats, and how do they feel your first five weeks have progressed?

During this week make sure you get on top of your day-to-day administration and clear as much of your in-box as possible. Ensure that your email list is in control, and take time to delegate non-critical tasks to members of the team as early as possible. Remember that it is much better to deal with issues early, before they become crises.

Week 7: Build your reputation

Recognise that your new role may be fundamentally different to your previous role, and that in order to succeed you may need to do things differently. This is particularly important when it is your first role in management, where you will have switched from achieving results through your own efforts and expertise to achieving results through others. Recognise that your personal reputation will now be dependent on the ability of the team to deliver results. Start to look outside your own organisation and identify industry best practices. Seek to understand how you compare with others and with the best of the competition, and what ideas you can and should adopt.

Think about the different events you attend on a week-to-week basis, and how you should behave on each occasion. Check that you need to attend these and if there are other meetings that might be more relevant. Think about what you can do to enhance your reputation as a performance management professional. Think about what you will get out of each event, but ask what you can do to contribute. Perhaps there are opportunities for you to take more of a leadership role, or to facilitate others.

Take time to build your network. The more senior you become, the more important your network will be to your future success. Your key contacts will initially be internal to the business, but as you become more established, look outside the business at professional bodies. Be critical in terms of how you use your time as some of the network organisations you can join promise a lot but deliver little, but as a performance management champion in the business seek to identify and bring in novel ideas, new thinking and best practices from other organisations.

Week 8: Build your team

Creating collaborations is frequently a shortcut to settling on your improvement plan. Prioritise those stakeholder relationships that will fast track your aims and goals. Put time in the diary to build those collaborative relationships and encourage your direct reports to do the same. At the same time keep your balance; make sure that you continue to keep things in perspective. If you have not done it already, prioritise time for yourself, your health and your family. This will allow you to maintain energy and keep your thinking sharp.

Don't forget that it a manager's job to support others to achieve their ambitions. You know the ambitions of others because you have already discovered them through your collaborations and conversations. Stay true to those discoveries; help your key stakeholders, peers and direct reports achieve their ambitions, and you will achieve your own.

Things to avoid These are the opposites to those listed above:

→ Avoid isolating yourself.

→ Avoid coming up with all the answers yourself; involve your team.

→ Avoid sticking too long with the existing team before making changes.

→ Avoid attempting too much too quickly.

→ Avoid being captured by the wrong people.

→ Avoid setting unrealistic expectations.

QUICK TIP **PERFORMANCE AUDIT**
Get into the habit of reviewing your team against the performance improvement audit on a regular basis (at least once a year).

Week 9: Reflect and learn

Now stop and review where you are. Take an hour or so at the start of the week to sit back and reflect on what has gone well, and what has gone badly, and why. Go back to your original plan or to-do list and check off the items you have delivered against, and critically review areas where you failed to meet expectations.

Meet with your boss and ask for an informal review of your progress. Many bosses are not very good at doing performance reviews, but nevertheless it is an essential part of continuous improvement. Then meet with your other stakeholders and get their inputs into what has gone well, and what they would like to see changed. Here's a good example of the benefits of this.

A new innovation champion in a drinks company ran an innovation workshop where 120 new ideas were generated over a two-day period. Everyone who attended the event enjoyed it and considered it a great success. However, just as she had put a lot of time into planning the event, she spent time seeking feedback from everyone who attended, and spent 15 minutes over coffee with key people across the business. She learned that the business thought that it was a worthwhile event, and that more should be held in the future. She also learned from her boss that the session needed to be more focused as the ideas were not aligned enough to current business imperatives, and that a couple of the functional managers were put out that they had not been invited. She was able to use these insights to plan future events that would generate better-quality ideas with a greater level of support from those functions that she needed for effective implementation.

Week 10: Develop your two-year plan

Over the last nine weeks you have built your reputation and credibility as team manager who has performance improvement high on their priorities list. You have developed important relationships with influential stakeholders, and your confidence has grown. You will by now have an opinion on what you want to achieve based on facts and the advice of experts around the business. Now is the time to develop your two-year plan, and seek to influence the strategic direction of the business. You will already have used some of the Fast Track top ten, and the time has come to finish the planning process off.

A lot will depend on whether you are starting from scratch or taking over an existing team, but in either case start by reflecting on your earlier vision and update it if necessary. Perhaps you can be more ambitious in implementing your strategic framework, or perhaps you want to focus on getting collaborative champions up and running in all functional teams. Then work back and identify what needs to be done and achieved on a month-by-month basis. Keep the plan for year 2 at a high level, but plan the first three months in detail.

Once you have your plan, identify barriers or potential problems that could get in your way. What could go wrong, what could cause this to happen, and what can you do to prevent it? Build these actions into the plan.

Finally, you should be as specific as possible about how you will know if you are succeeding. Set key performance indicators (KPIs) that you can monitor on a month-to-month basis that will let you and your boss know if you are on track. Make sure that at least one indicator tracks the financial benefits of your work, what some people refer to as the return on investment (RoI), as this will help you to justify future investment in you and your team.

QUICK TIP *IDEAS DATABASE*

Set up a simple database of performance improvement ideas for your team. Start with a simple spreadsheet or whiteboard, classify each idea as to whether it is a major new insight of continuous improvement or not, and make sure that something happens to each idea.

Checklist

What do I need to know?

During your first ten weeks in a new job start gathering information that will help you to deliver results, build your team and develop your career. Use this checklist to see if you have the necessary information – using a simple Red-Amber-Green status where Red = major gaps in current knowledge and immediate action is required, Amber = some knowledge is missing and may need to be addressed at some stage in the future, and Green means that you are on track.

TOPIC	INFORMATION	RAG
Business context	The major trends inside and outside the industry that will impact what you do, how you do it and your performance enhancement priorities	
Business strategy	The overall strategy for the business in terms of its products and markets and the basis on which it differentiates itself in the market	
Team objectives	The KPIs that will be used to assess whether you and your team have been a success	
Stakeholders	Those individuals or groups that you will work with and that will influence success or failure of your innovation activities	
The team	Individual members of your team – their names, their backgrounds and their relative strengths and weaknesses	
Roles	Defined roles and responsibilities needed to deliver results – internal to the team or external contributors	

TOPIC	INFORMATION	RAG
Customers	Your top five internal or external customers and their specific must-haves and wants	
Suppliers	Your top ten suppliers – who they are and how they contribute to the success of your team	
Your boss	Your operational manager – who they are, their preferred style, and what it is that really makes them tick	
The director	The person most committed to performance management activities within the business, and possibly the person whose job you aspire to	
Key opinion leaders	People across the organisation whose expert knowledge and opinion is respected by others – who they are and what they each have to offer	
Current commitments	The current operational activities – what they are and what it will take to succeed	
Future workload	Future expectations in terms of what needs to be delivered when and by whom	
Budget	The amount of funding available for your activities – where this will come from and what the sign-off process is	
Resources	The people, facilities, equipment, materials and information available to you for all your activities	
Scope	The boundaries that have been set for you and your team – the things you are not allowed to do	
Key events	The major events that are happening within the business that will influence what you need to do and when	
Potential problems	The risks you face going forward – the things that could go wrong based on the assumptions you have made	
SWOT	The relative strengths, weaknesses, opportunities and threats for your team	
Review process	The formal review process for your internal team reviews, and where KPIs will be reviewed with your boss	

QUICK TIP CONSTRUCTIVE CHALLENGE
Get into the habit of challenging members of your team to think differently, to explore options and to build their case for new ways of doing things.

STOP – THINK – ACT

Now put together a plan for your first ten weeks:

What should I do?	What do I need to achieve?
Who do I need to involve?	Who needs to be involved and why?
What resources will I require?	What information, facilities, materials, equipment of budget will be required?
What is the timing?	When will tasks be achieved?
	Week 1
	Week 2
	Week 3
	Week 4
	Week 5
	Week 6
	Week 7
	Week 8
	Week 9
	Week 10

Visit **www.Fast-Track-Me.com** to use the Fast Track online planning tool.

Managing people the Socratic way

Dr Serge Besanger, ESSEC Asia-Pacific

Encouraging a Socratic style of management allows executives to create teams that think innovatively without deviating from corporate missions and objectives. Socratic managers empower their employees through open conversation and creative questioning, generally letting them figure out solutions by themselves. A key to genuine Socratic people-management is to often suspend judgement and comment, thereby enabling team dialogue and collectively creating innovative solutions.

EXPERT VOICE

EXPERT VOICE

Great Britain's most prominent example of a successful Socratic leader constantly challenging his team is Winston Churchill. During World War II, Churchill would often let forth impractical battle proposals to elicit critical feedback and creative counterproposals from his officers, and the creative thinking led to Britain's victory.

Here is a series of guidelines that would help you ask questions in an uncoerced manner:

1 Display naivety when asking questions.

2 Ask for the other party's opinion and allow them to expose their personal beliefs and doctrines on the situation.

3 Never lose patience when listening.

4 Devise a series of clever analogies aimed at shaking the foundations of that person's doctrine.

5 Let the other party naturally realise the futility of their arguments by perhaps answering with silence or frowning slightly, but do not exploit puzzlement in a way that could cause loss of face. Never say: 'See, I told you so' or 'I'm always right'.

6 Guide the other party to the rightful conclusion.

7 Let the other party claim ownership of it.

7

LEADING THE TEAM

Leadership is as important to success as gaining expert knowledge and being familiar with appropriate tools and techniques. Focus on your personal attributes as a leader in a new situation and reflect on what it takes to lead and develop a team.

The right thinking

How should I think?

The starting point is to look closely at yourself and reflect on your self-perception. If you are a newly promoted manager or have just been made a team leader, make sure you review that self-perception and adjust it where necessary. As you get into more challenging jobs, you must move onwards and upwards in your thinking.

All roles are different by nature, but the jump from one grade to the next is probably the most pronounced when you first step into management. How often do we hear people reflecting on how the ace sales representative does not necessarily make the best sales manager? This is the same for any leader. You may have been great at delivering the required results excellently, but can you get others to do the same, and can you lead and motivate a team of people that may not even report to you using only influence and charisma?

Whilst you are probably excited by the new challenge, it is not some-thing you do for the fun of it – you've got to make money. Whatever function you are involved in, you must drive results to the bottom line.

You will also need to be more aware of the whole organisation, and be proactive in terms of anticipating change. How much time do you spend thinking about the future; is it really enough? One of the key attributes of the Fast Track manager is that they will spend more time looking up and around them at what is happening in other functions or businesses.

QUICK TIP YOUR NEXT JOB

Think about your next job and imagine how different it will be, then list the things you can do today to help prepare for this next challenge.

What personal attributes will I need?

The starting point for managing an effective team is to manage yourself. Whenever I see a manager setting career and personal development activities and plans for members of their team, I am often impressed by their professionalism. Unfortunately, all too often they have not been so diligent with their own personal development planning.

Conducting a self-assessment against four dimensions – knowledge, competencies, attitudes and behaviours – is a useful starting point. Do you have the necessary knowledge about changes in the industry, your top ten customers and major competitors? Are you able to think creatively, con-duct analyses to understand why things happen (or could happen), review all processes and put into place plans that will deliver benefits on time and within budget? Do you have the right attitude in terms of being positive, seeking synergies between other people's ideas and constantly looking for breakthroughs? And do you actively support others in doing their jobs and have the determination to overcome obstacles?

Use a structured approach to identify specific areas in each of four categories that you need to work on: knowledge, competencies, attitudes and behaviours. However, before taking action, take time to discuss your thoughts with your boss or your coach and seek evidence for good or poor performance. Perhaps summarise your thoughts in the form of a

SWOT (strengths, weaknesses, opportunities and threats) analysis before putting a plan together. However, do not be over-ambitious and try and develop yourself too quickly – becoming an effective team manager takes time.

> **QUICK TIP BUSINESS STRATEGY**
> Make sure you know what the strategy of your business is, and focus your activities on the specific imperatives for the next one to three years.

The right skills

What leadership style is appropriate?

The purpose of this section is to provide a road map of how to recognise the need for different leadership styles depending upon the situation the team and the business is facing. This is commonly known as 'situational leadership'. Situational leadership identifies the situation the team is in and enables the leader to adapt the style of leadership to suit that situation.

In this section we will look at:

→ Styles of leadership and purpose of those styles in relation to the 'situation'

→ Three key competencies central to leadership style

→ Evaluating where you are now and where you need to be to achieve your aspirations.

Styles of leadership and the purpose of those styles in relation to the 'situation'
(The styles have been numbered in order to match the quick assessment process later in this section.)

Style level 1 'chain of command' In the chain of command style, the leader makes and announces all decisions whilst also directing each person's activities. There is limited communication other than on immediate tasks and minimal autonomy for team members. The team is very closed and will rarely draw in expertise from outside, instead focusing on individual areas of responsibility.

This style is very associated with the army, where there is no room for negotiation or for individuals to act outside the series of tasks and roles required of them. When a company is going through financial crisis and restructure, this kind of rigidity and control is desirable in order to be able to survive.

Style level 2 'leader is central' When leaders are central, they are critical hubs for team communication, decision making and performance. While the leader may ask for ideas, they almost always make the decisions. The leader manages everyone's activities whilst individuals are limited to their own tasks.

An example of a situation where this style is appropriate is where a leader is project managing a team where team members are moving in and out of the project and the team project leader needs to be the one holding the 'golden thread' of consistency.

Style level 3 'transition' In terms of team development this team is in a 'transition phase'. Team members have begun to select and organise their own work, only reporting results to the leader. The leader is concerned with promoting teamwork, cooperation and communication among members and is still central in facilitating change. Some members may be more empowered than others.

Here is a team that is on the road to maturity, where some individuals are able to take responsibility and are empowered through their capabilities, talent and ability to act on their own within the overall framework. These individuals are collaborating and in cooperation with each other in pursuit of the results.

Style level 4 'leadership is shared' The leader is both facilitator and coach. They may still make some decisions (e.g. selection of team members) and be involved in coordination, but in effect the 'leadership is shared'. The group decides inputs, outputs and almost all aspects of the work (e.g. training, work rosters campaigns, structure and plans for projects). The group structure is not rigid and flexes according to the goals. This is the structure for a high-performing team, where all team members work on shared goals that they have been engaged in agreeing. The team understands and is able to work with the diverse personalities that give it breadth, flexibility and capability. There is collaboration, unification and cohesion. The leader facilitates that level of cooperation, engagement and overall direction. The leader coaches the team members to be able to perform as a team both collectively and individually.

Style level 5 'empowered teams' The 'empowered teams are completely self-directed. The leader coaches and supports several teams simultaneously, with the actual team responsible for all aspects of the group's operation (including administrative and personnel functions, such as recruitment and performance management). The group will also draw upon outside expertise while maintaining high levels of autonomy.

This scenario could apply to a global marketing function where there are four or five functional teams reporting in to a marketing director. This requires a level of organisational maturity that will have been grown through the previous style levels.

Three key competencies central to leadership style
The three competencies central to these styles are:

→ decision making

→ communication

→ performance management.

This is shown diagramatically below.

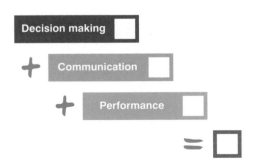

What follows are the descriptors for each competency matched to the style levels.

Decision making

Style level 1. All of the decisions are made by the leader with limited, if any, discussion with the team. The leader will always communicate the decisions without discussion using, for example, memos and briefings. The leader maintains tight control through all aspects of decision making and control.

Style level 2. The leader may ask for ideas from the team occasionally, but almost always makes all of the decisions alone. The leader provides members with limited autonomy to make decisions in their areas, but ensures there are clear processes to obtain their approval to a decision.

Style level 3. While the leader is still central in decision making, they do empower key team members to influence this process. The leader is responsible for facilitating change and will provide direction, strategy and vision. The leader is aware of all decisions made.

Style level 4. The leader makes some decisions (e.g. the selection of team members) and largely enables group responsibility for most of the decision making as defined within the structure of the strategic framework.

Style level 5. The leader enables the team to be responsible for all aspects of decision making. That includes day-to-day functions of the group as well as administration and personnel functions. The leader supports and empowers members to achieve this level of decision making.

Communication

Style level 1. There is limited communication from the leader to the team. Team members rarely communicate directly with the leader other than on immediate tasks. The leader does not use a variety of modes and channels or facilitate members to improve their communication.

Style level 2. The leader is the hub for communication between team members. Because of the approach, limited communication occurs directly with other members; instead, communication is via the leader using, for example, memos and emails. The leader keeps control of information flow.

Style level 3. Whilst it is necessary to report results to the leader, team members are encouraged to communicate directly to each other where appropriate. The leader enables team members to be somewhat autonomous and still may prefer structured communication.

Style level 4. Leaders coordinate communication in a facilitative manner. They allow members to draw in people from outside the group where necessary, using multiple channels and communicating autonomously.

Style level 5. The leader has facilitated exceptional communication patterns. They enable the team to communicate independently of centralised structures, utilising many modes and channels and directly to all relevant parties. Members are trained to be exceptional communicators.

Performance

Style level 1. The leader is involved with every aspect of an individual's activities. The leadership limits team members from interacting with others, instead engaging with tasks only set by the leader. Performance management is achieved at a micro level from top down.

Style level 2. The leader manages every member's individual tasks closely and does not necessarily promote teamwork. Instead, individuals are limited to their own tasks as set by the leader. The leader sees performance management as something requiring reasonable control.

Style level 3. The leader has developed the group to begin selecting and organising its own work. The leader's role is largely to promote an efficient environment, characterised by cooperation and strong teamwork. Under the leader's oversight, the team performs well.

Style level 4. The leader is a coach to the group and still may provide some direction concerning the way the team works and what activities members engage in. The team is mostly self-directed but still has input from the leader. The leader works to help the team improve performance.

Style level 5. The leader may not be involved with the day-to-day tasks or coordination of the group's performance. They have created a team that is highly self-directed and instead focus their leadership role as a coach to support several teams simultaneously.

Evaluating where you are now and where you need to be to achieve your aspirations

Using the numbers allocated to each descriptor in the three competency sections, decide which descriptor most accurately represents your current style. For example: in decision making I score 2, in communication it's a 3 and in performance management it's a 2. My overall score is therefore $2+3+2=7$.

Take the score and compare it with the range of scores in the grid opposite. As in the example above, my score puts me in the range of 5–7 which is 'leader is central.'

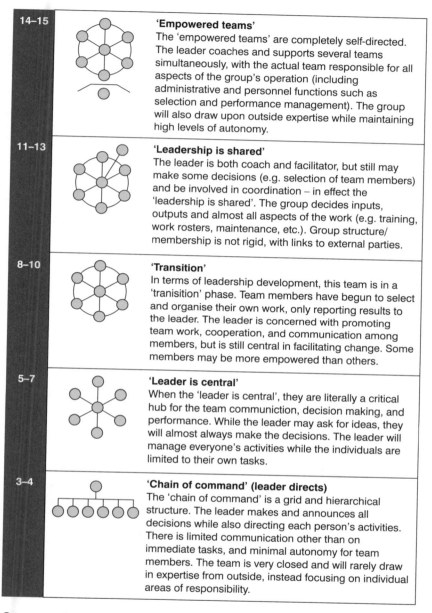

14–15		'**Empowered teams**'
		The 'empowered teams' are completely self-directed. The leader coaches and supports several teams simultaneously, with the actual team responsible for all aspects of the group's operation (including administrative and personnel functions such as selection and performance management). The group will also draw upon outside expertise while maintaining high levels of autonomy.
11–13		'**Leadership is shared**'
		The leader is both coach and facilitator, but still may make some decisions (e.g. selection of team members) and be involved in coordination – in effect the 'leadership is shared'. The group decides inputs, outputs and almost all aspects of the work (e.g. training, work rosters, maintenance, etc.). Group structure/membership is not rigid, with links to external parties.
8–10		'**Transition**'
		In terms of leadership development, this team is in a 'tranisition' phase. Team members have begun to select and organise their own work, only reporting results to the leader. The leader is concerned with promoting team work, cooperation, and communication among members, but is still central in facilitating change. Some members may be more empowered than others.
5–7		'**Leader is central**'
		When the 'leader is central', they are literally a critical hub for the team communiction, decision making, and performance. While the leader may ask for ideas, they will almost always make the decisions. The leader will manage everyone's activities while the individuals are limited to their own tasks.
3–4		'**Chain of command**' (leader directs)
		The 'chain of command' is a grid and hierarchical structure. The leader makes and announces all decisions while also directing each person's activities. There is limited communication other than on immediate tasks, and minimal autonomy for team members. The team is very closed and will rarely draw in expertise from outside, instead focusing on individual areas of responsibility.

Once you have understood your current style ask yourself if, given the goals and purpose of this team, that style is appropriate and if not what is the style you need to develop yourself and the team towards. This should correlate with the high-performing team assessment.

Coaching

Whilst not part of the formal leadership model above, coaching should play a role in developing yourself as well as members of your team. It is said that if you want to master a particular discipline then teach it. Fast Track managers develop excellent coaching skills helping individuals develop core skills or resolve problems. They in turn are prepared and willing to be coached.

CASE STORY *INTERNATIONAL HOTEL CHAIN, PETER'S STORY*

Narrator Peter is an international sales training consultant in the leisure industry.

Context An international hotel chain was trying to increase its conference business, concentrating on corporate customers who it had previously treated only as 'short-stay' guests. In most of the hotels the conference facilities were new annexes added on principally to offer wedding facilities at the weekends, so this would be a good use of the facilities mid-week.

Issue The chain hired an international sales training consultant whose brief was to train all the national sales forces to sell the new conference package. However, she was not familiar with the traditions and cultures of the regions and countries, and whilst all the salespeople were meant to be fluent in English, in reality a large proportion had very limited language skills. The result was that many were confused by the training and either no change to their behaviour occurred or the effect of the training wore off quite quickly.

Solution The company decided on a new approach to training and appointed external consultants not to do the training but to provide the materials for local managers to use in regular coaching sessions with their team. They only trained a few people in each country who then adapted the materials to local customs and ran weekly coaching sessions for their people at a set time every week.

Furthermore the company integrated a sales template with an online coach so that new and inexperienced sales people and managers could get up to speed quickly.

Learning The training became effective because the managers became much more skilled in coaching their own people in their own cultures. Sales of conference centre facilities during the following weeks rose steadily.

QUICK TIP NETWORK FOR PERFORMANCE IMPROVEMENT
Use your network and that of your team, as ideas for improvement often come from outside the workplace.

The right environment

What culture is best?

There is no one right answer to this, and it will vary depending on your preferred style and the business context or situation at a point in time. However, there are basic components that tend to result in an environment that will be more conducive to creating high-performing teams.

Creative challenge

Create an environment of challenge and confrontation, but make sure that it is positive. It is easy to knock an idea, but make sure when you or a member of the team does that, you have an alternative or are prepared to search for one. As an example, an experienced team leader talks about the three roles that people could fulfil when taking part in planning workshops – called the 3 Ts. Ideally, she is keen to get people to think about ways in which they could transform the team – finding new ways of changing the organisation's culture to influence the way people act and think: **the transformers**. However, the reality is that some people turn up for a day away from the day job, possibly off-site with their friends and a nice meal – she calls these the **tourists**. The third T are the people who always have other things to be doing, 1,000 emails to be getting on with and are also intent on finding the day a complete waste of time – she refers to these people as **terrorists!** By making these three roles explicit at the beginning of the workshop, she is able to get most of the team to focus on being transformers.

Blame-free

When generating ideas for cultural change, there is always a degree of uncertainty and risk. This means that people will not always get it right, and not all ideas will be good ideas. Where ideas are heavily criticised, people quickly stop putting forward new concepts for fear of being ridiculed. Here's a good, and real, example of this. A project manager in a software consultancy put forward an idea for a new computer system that would potentially help their customers to steal a march on their competition. However, after nine months and $10 million in capital investment, the software was pronounced a failure and withdrawn from the portfolio. Two weeks later the executive was called in to see the CEO at a board meeting. Fearing the worst, he apologised to the board, and stated that he fully understood if they'd called him in to 'let him go'. To his surprise, the CEO stated, 'Let you go? We've just spent $10 million educating you – why would we let you go?' The key is obviously to accept that new ideas are about the future, and the future is uncertain – be prepared, indeed encourage people, to take risks and make mistakes.

Ethics and governance

Make a choice about what you will and what you will not be prepared to consider. As well as making a statement about your beliefs – what is right, and what is wrong – you will also clarify the boundaries for others. When Nokia moved into downloadable software games for its handsets, the project team looking at new ideas for this emerging market were told very clearly *not* to look at games involving gambling. In any industry there will be the possibility of cutting corners, flirting with legality and, for example, behaving in a more or less green manner. Think about the issues that affect you and your industry and make decisions on the limits you will set. This is particularly relevant when dealing with developing economies.

Learning organisation

Work hard to create a culture where people learn from each other and from the past. There is nothing more demoralising than coming out with a new idea that fails badly to achieve new stretching goals, only to find that someone else had already made the very same mistake several years earlier. This is a discipline that needs to be built into the culture of the team. For example, a Japanese mobile phone manufacturer developed a new phone that combined advanced software with the latest thin screen technology to create a display that was second to none. Unfortunately, once released it quickly became clear that the mechanism for embedding the display in the phone was faulty, and almost 50 per cent of the phones had to be recalled. This cost the business approximately $5 million in rejects and $5 million in terms of the adverse impact on the brand. But in the spirit of the blame-free culture, the senior management team stated that this was understandable for a leading technology company – there would be some failures. However, nine months later the upgrade to the phone was released, and whilst it had some highly new features, it still had the same fault as the original phone. At this point the senior management team came together and agreed that an effective means of capturing and sharing 'lessons learned' was needed!

Building the team

What makes a great team?

So you have a great leadership style that is flexible enough to cope with different situations, and you have a number of highly motivated and skilled people to work with, but that does not necessarily make them a great team. So what do the successful teams do that differentiates them from average performers? Read through the following summary checklist, and reflect on what you need to do as leader of the team in order to ensure success.

→ **The team will have great clarity in its goals and have a real sense of shared purpose**. Fast Track teams will have such clarity of vision that they will know how they want to be remembered long after they have been disbanded.

→ **The team will have a strong and enthusiastic leader** who provides direction, is supportive of team members and willing to shoulder responsibility when things do not go according to plan. They are often not the expert or specialist, but they understand how to bring experts together and get them to perform effectively as a unit. Members will be empowered to take action, and be willing to take on the leadership role themselves as and when required.

→ **Fast Track teams also accept that things will change, and have an ability to accept this and be flexible in order to bring things back on track**. Perhaps a project team is implementing a major change programme, and within the first week a key member of the team leaves. They will reappraise the situation quickly but calmly, explore creative options for dealing with the situation and move on.

→ **The team will have shared values and a common set of operating principles**. Whilst teams comprise people with a variety of skills and experiences, they need to be unified by common beliefs. We see the enormous power that the adoption of a common set of religious beliefs can have for both positive and negative, and whilst levels of fanaticism are rarely positive, shared values will often provide the team with enormous energy and commitment.

→ **Ideally, the shared values then extend into a general respect and liking for each other where members of the team trust each other and genuinely have fun working together**. The Armed Forces will always ensure that their teams spend time gaining shared experiences together in a safe environment before they are asked to put their lives on the line.

→ There will be issues to deal with, but the Fast Track teams will manage these quickly and sensitively before they become crises. To do this they need to have open and honest communication, and work in a blame-free environment where rewards for success are shared.

→ Whilst these teams will focus on their primary objectives, they will have a feeling of shared responsibility and be supportive of each other. They will take time out to continuously learn and develop new skills – both individually and as a team. This necessitates keeping an eye on how they are performing, and scanning other similar teams in order to identify alternative approaches that could be adopted.

Finally, the team will be balanced in terms of the skills and capabilities of team members, and in terms of the roles they each fulfil. They have people capable of creative challenge, but they also need people willing to get their heads down in order to put in the work and deliver the results.

How should I develop the team?

As well as developing the skills of individual members of your team, you need to build them into a team. Review the list of attributes of a great team above, and make a note of any area where you feel there is a need for improvement.

Next, assess where you think the team is now in terms of their stage of development. This is particularly important for those working in the area of innovation, as teams are often part-time – coming together for events such as innovation workshops or implementation of an initiative. Each team will go through various stages of development, and your role as the leader will be to recognise where members are, and to take action to move them to a state where members are their most productive. Consider the model overleaf:[1]

---

[1] Concept developed by Bruce Wayne Tuckman in the short article 'Development sequence in small groups', 1965, *Psychological Bulletin*, 63(6), pp. 384–99 (Naval Medical Research Institute, Bethesda, MD).

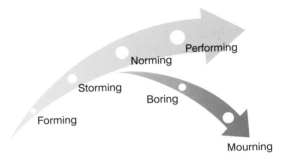

STAGE	DESCRIPTION	LEADERSHIP ACTIONS
Forming	The group is brought together for the first time, and needs to spend time understanding each other and what they are each contributing. This is typical of a focused innovation workshop that comprises members from a variety of functions that do not usually work together, but it will also happen with implementation teams.	Think carefully about whom to involve in each team and make sure there is a balance in terms of different roles, skills and experience. Allow people to get to know each other personally, and set simple tasks to allow people to work together for the first time and get a quick win.
Storming	Initially they will each be keen to contribute, and will want to have their say in terms of who fulfils which role and who will have the greatest sway over the outcomes. If this is not managed carefully, teams can become very 'political' where individuals jockey for power and positions. This can result in a downward spiral in terms of effectiveness.	Make sure that the early tasks the team undertakes are straightforward and will result in success. Establish team roles and communicate them clearly so that everyone knows what their contribution is. There will always be the potential for conflict, so look for it, and seek consensus on key decisions at an early stage.
Norming	As the group settles down, the team needs to adopt norms in terms of how they work together. This needs to cover decision making, communication and meeting disciplines. Without common processes a lot of the energy and enthusiasm of the team can be dissipated.	Be clear about what will happen at each meeting, and that there are agreed objectives, an agenda with timings and appropriate resources. Communicate your leadership style in terms of the circumstances in which you will seek the team's views.

STAGE	DESCRIPTION	LEADERSHIP ACTIONS
Performing	The team should now have clear roles, and be working effectively as a unit. This is where results are produced, and you need to keep the team in this positive and effective mode.	Monitor performance regularly, and take swift action to resolve issues before they become crises. Spend one-to-one time with each member of the team to keep them motivated.
Boring	For teams that have been together for a long time, there is a danger that they stop challenging the way they work. This is common on major projects where individuals can easily get into a rut. If left unnoticed, it can result in the team getting bored, and performance can quickly fall off.	Find ways of constantly challenging the team as a whole and as individuals. Consider bringing in new members, or rotate jobs and roles. Perhaps, there will come a point where you need to fundamentally adjust the team's objectives in order to get them to stop and re-evaluate what they are doing.
Mourning	Finally, for high-performing teams, there is always a major sense of loss when a valued member moves on. Even if their replacement appears to have the right profile, there can be resistance, and the team effectively moves back into the 'forming' stage.	When people leave the team, for good or bad reasons, think carefully about the transition. Focus on some of the softer people issues within the team – not simply on updating the plan.

The processes for going through these stages are described in Chapter 3.

How do I overcome barriers to change?

Performance management is all about change. New ideas relating to the business DNA, to creating high-performing teams, and to managing performance using the leadership dashboard to produce a high-performing team will all require that you change people's jobs and attitudes. Recognise that the ideas you and your team generate may be worthwhile, but accept that there will be resistance simply because some people do not like change. The denial, resistance, exploration, commitment (DREC) change model – see the figure overleaf – can help you understand the process that people need to go through, and give insights in terms of what you will need to consider when planning changes.

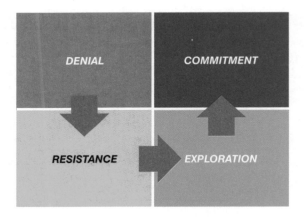

→ **Denial.** People believe that the current situation is perfectly acceptable and refuse to accept that the change is needed or that change will happen. Perhaps the innovation is to shut down the customer services department and outsource it to a specialist company, or overseas. You hear the cry of 'It will never happen' coming from different teams. Most organisations regularly fail to implement changes effectively, and the organisation reverts back to its former state quite quickly. It is perhaps no wonder that people are often cynical and will wait to see if anything actually happens. To be taken seriously you have to drive the change through. Accept that some people will be in denial, but find a way of helping them to come to terms with the fact that the change will happen.

→ **Resistance.** Even when people have accepted that the change will happen, many will still be resistant. It is their way of telling you that they are still not convinced that this is the right way to go. Work out counter-arguments in advance, take time to explain the business case for the change, and make it clear why the current situation will not endure. Identify those people in the business who have bought in to the idea and who are also widely respected: we call these people the key opinion leaders (KOLs). Use these people to spread the word and explain to others why this change is so vital for the future. Experience has shown that if 20 per cent of KOLs are positive about the change you will probably be able to drive it through; with less than that you may have difficult problems to overcome.

→ **Exploration.** Once there is an acceptance that the change will happen and that it is a good thing, allow people to investigate ways in which it will impact them, their own and other teams for the better, and ways in which they can help with implementation. Get them involved, allow them to ask questions and make sure they are taking action.

→ **Commitment.** Finally, as they start to realise the benefits, take time to capture the early victories, write them up and communicate them across other teams. Often, those that showed the greatest level of resistance, once converted, become your best advocates!

The DREC cycle is a useful way of understanding the natural stages we all go through when faced with change. Some of us will move through the cycle much faster than others, so take time early on to help those that are struggling to move through the cycle.

QUICK TIP COMMUNICATING BENEFITS
Don't bore people with minute details and lists of tasks, but focus on what is important and the unique selling proposition of the idea.

STOP – THINK – ACT
Reflect on how well you are leading the team and look for ways you could improve. Now think about how well the team is operating and where the team is in the forming to mourning model? What groups affected by the change are not in the 'committed' section of the DREC model?

What should we do?	What actions do we need to take to build the team?
Who do we need to involve?	Who needs to be involved and why?
What resources will we require?	What level of investment would be required?
What is the timing?	What deadlines do we need to meet?

Visit **www.Fast-Track-Me.com** to use the Fast Track online planning tool.

Creating a learning organisation

Professor Mike Pedler Henley Business School, University of Reading

Reg Revans's[2] ecological formula is L ≥ C. This holds that learning (L) in any organism, from simple cells to complex human organisations, must equal or exceed the rate of change (C), otherwise they will be in decline, falling behind the times and failing to advance and thrive.

Organisations start as ideas in the heads of people. When they are young, they tend to be busy, active places, full of natural learning. As they get older, and as the founders grow weary or the original markets decline, that vital working and learning energy can drain away and get lost. The learning organisation idea is about making conscious efforts to innovate, rejuvenate and redevelop this energy. This is done through encouraging learning in individuals, teams, networks and even whole organisations: 'A learning company is an organisation that facilitates the learning of all its members and consciously transforms itself and its context.'[3]

Learning and performance

Today there are huge pressures on leadership to deliver demanding performance goals, to deal with high levels of environmental change and to innovate – all at the same time. The Holy Grail is the performance culture that is also a learning culture, where people are encouraged to pursue results energetically and also to learn from their experience by continuous open and critical review.

Can these two be done together? This is a 'big ask' indeed. The benefits of performance management are well publicised, but the downsides are also obvious and widespread. How can we manage performance without making people target-obsessed, conservative, risk-averse, closed and defensive? The capacity and willingness to learn is easily crushed. People who are fearful or not respected do not learn; people who are not challenged do not learn; and people who are not encouraged and supported do not learn. Leadership must create the processes, structures,

---

[2] Reg Revans was the founder for Action Learning. He introduced the concept in the mid-1940s as Director of Education for the National Coal Board. He continued to promote and develop its principles until his death in 2003. His Action Learning concept is now used by various organisations throughout the world.

[3] Pedler, M., Burgoyne, J. and Boydell, T. (1997) *The Learning Company: A Strategy for Sustainable Development*, Maidenhead: McGraw-Hill, p.3.

cultures and relationships that balance performance with development and innovation to protect this precious capacity for learning – see the see-saw of performance and learning below.

Paths to learning and innovation

This balancing act is attempted in different ways. The philosophy of one organisation I know can be summed up as: 'Meeting your targets gives you headroom for development'.

What is the philosophy in your organisation? In my travels I have found different people and places interpreting the learning organisation idea in marvellously diverse ways. Here are four stories, all responses to the question: 'How is your business a learning organisation?'

→ 'In this company we have declared that we are going to be a learning organisation. Not only this but that we are going to be a world class learning organisation! We have a "learning table" at lunchtimes – where you can have a free lunch but you have to talk about learning in some way to the other people you find there.'

→ 'I am the Medical Director in a University Hospital. The hospital is full of different professional groups – doctors, nurses, therapists, researchers, technicians of many varieties – and this can be bad for patients. We started a disease management programme and all the professionals learned to define this process together. This is a seed for a new learning culture.'

→ 'To us being a learning organisation means sustainability. A manager I know wanted to develop his people but had little money. So he made his poor performers redundant and made a considerable investment in training the others. Customer satisfaction went from 60 per cent to 90 per cent, but how do you sustain this?'

→ 'For ten years I was the manager in a publishing company; I then left to become a wife and mother at home. After some time I got in touch with a local organisation that helps people to learn to deal with themselves and others in a development process. Now, with seven others whom I met, we are going back to work in profit and non-profit organisations. We always work in pairs to evaluate our work. We have four meetings a year to share and help each other.'

EXPERT VOICE

Is this giving you any ideas? There are many paths and, on the principle that 'the wisdom to fix this business resides within', it is important to work out what might work for you and your colleagues, and what might be sustained.

Leadership, learning and innovation are closely connected. Following new paths leads to exploration, discovery and learning. In the learning organisation, leadership can be defined as *learning on behalf of the organisation*.

8

GETTING TO THE TOP

Finally, think about what you need to do to stand out amongst your peers, stay current and then to get ahead. As you progress up the corporate ladder you need to continuously focus on managing performance for maximum results, and increasingly look up and out as opposed to in and down. Your personal network will be more and more important, and you will need to start to think and act like a director.

Focus on performance

Fast Track managers know what is important and what is not, and focus on the key performance indicators (KPIs) that have the greatest impact on what they are trying to achieve. At all times they understand where they are now, what the bottlenecks are and how to clear them. They regularly take time to look around for best practice, to reflect on the past in order to learn from what went well or what could be improved on, and to think ahead to the future so that concerns can be resolved before they become crises. By always delivering against expectations, they stand out from the pack and will be automatic considerations for promotion at the appropriate time.

Performance snapshot: past – historic

There is a universal complaint from historians that politicians don't learn from the lessons of history. This tends to be true of businesses as well. Without a clear understanding of what has happened before, we risk repeating mistakes from the past, or reacting to a crisis that doesn't actually exist – fixing what's not broke. There was an engineering company, for example, with a poor record for delivering on time and within budget. Its poor past performance may have been undesirable, but the complete lack of competition meant that it was not in crisis; it could improve performance over time without the extra costs involved in treating the situation as a crisis. When it brought new talent on to the board, the new boy made it quite clear that this was not a long-term strategy and insisted that the company review and improve its delivery results. 'Eventually,' he argued, 'someone else will come into the market and interrupt your satisfaction with a poor record.'

So, review your KPIs and assess how well you performed in the last period, what the trend was, and perhaps what the specific problems were. This goes into the information pot for the next version of the plan.

Many organisations maintain a lessons-learned database but then rarely use it. The trouble is that they are easy to set up, but difficult to allow easy access to for the people who you want to reach. After all, such a database is an important, commercially sensitive asset. Think about how you, in your situation, could find out about what has happened before.

For example, during a project management training session in a large manufacturing company, the participants were asked how they ensured they learned from previous mistakes. They stated that it took them two days to identify databases that may contain useful information, another two days to get security clearance to look at the data, and even then the data was unstructured and next to useless. Once the manager had left the room, they all admitted that they just didn't bother anymore and started with a blank piece of paper.

Performance snapshot: present – current situation (gap)

The organisation's managers have to focus on the right priorities. If they don't, then they risk turning a problem into a crisis. They will want to know:

→ what is currently going on, what projects are underway and what operational teams are doing

→ whether or not projects and teams are on track and, if not,

→ what are the issues and who is dealing with them?

They want this information in a specific way, not as a series of vague intentions. They might use the SMART acronym by saying they want information on results that is specific, measurable, accurate, relevant and timely.

Performance snapshot: future – predictive

KPIs tend to focus on what has happened historically (just as a profit and loss account will tell you how the business performed in the last reporting period). Check that your KPIs are looking in all three directions – current and future as well as past. You will want to be sure that your pipeline of ideas is still aligned to the current business imperatives as these will often change throughout the year.

Think about risks and risk management. Constantly reassess which teams are likely to fail so that you can be ready to deal with the casualties – both the performance gap and the people working on them.

Invite challenge

Who can we get to challenge us?

Fast Track managers never rest on their laurels. You may think that your performance is on track, but as the external business environment changes you need to adapt. Look for ways to introduce challenge to yourself and your team on a regular basis, aiming to bring in ideas, tools and techniques from recognised business leaders. Review the different groups (see the figure overleaf):

→ **Other internal teams:** What ideas can be shared? What common risks can be avoided?

→ **Customers:** How are their must-haves, needs and wants changing? What future scenarios might occur?

→ **Competitors:** What are they doing now that could be copied ('swiped' or reverse engineered)?

→ **Supply chain:** What possibilities are there for improved effectiveness and efficiency?

→ **Partners:** What can we learn from them? What opportunities are there for collaboration?

→ **Industry advisers:** What are the experts recommending? What breakthrough tools and techniques have they developed?

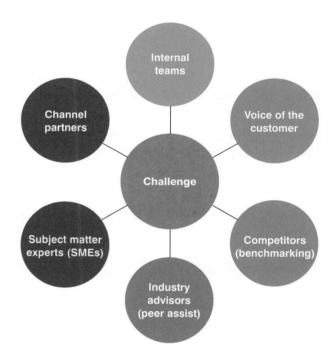

Engage in challenging acts on a regular basis even if you don't need to in order to meet your KPIs because you're ahead of the game. If you are finding it easy to meet the targets set for you, then don't wait for your boss to make them more stretching, do it yourself. Perhaps take time to get involved in areas where you are not confident in order to continuously develop yourself.

Remember to use relevant opportunities for self-development both inside and outside work, within your function and without. Consider the following:

→ Get involved in public speaking, such as working on internal management development courses.

→ Commission external studies by using undergraduate students, for example.

→ Get involved in an outside body involved with strategic issues relating to your function.

→ Get on the steering committee of a professional institute.

→ Respond to public enquires (from the government) and try to get on review bodies by developing a specialism or positive reputation.

→ Get experience of board work through acting in the role in a company spin-out or increase your exposure to your own company board and its way of thinking by making presentations when the opportunity arises.

→ Get on internal working parties investigating company issues but possibly outside the innovation project area.

How do I keep up to date?

As well as working with other groups inside and outside of the business, think carefully about what additional sources of knowledge and insight you want to receive and how often. There is a wealth of information available from a variety of sources, so you need to be selective as the time you have available for reading is limited and the quality can be variable.

→ **Web:** provides freely available information from a variety of sources, but is typically unstructured and will contain bias. *Fast Track recommendation*: review the websites of your 'top ten' customers and competitors twice a year, and identify up to five other useful websites that provide challenge.

→ **Journals or trade magazines:** available via a subscription and will make the latest ideas and thinking available but will often contain a lot of commercial advertorials. *Fast Track recommendation*: subscribe to the one journal of greatest relevance to your industry for one year and review its value. Once you have read it, make sure you circulate it to other members of your team.

→ **Conferences and exhibitions:** provide a useful opportunity to listen to stimulating presentations and are typically an excellent way of networking with others outside the business, but can be time-consuming and expensive. *Fast Track recommendation*: identify the one conference of greatest relevance to your industry and attend it for two consecutive years. Aim to identify at least three people (other attendees or presenters) to follow up with about specific issues you have.

→ **Communities of practice:** online discussion forums between like-minded people within the innovation community. *Fast Track recommendation*: these can be extremely useful or a complete waste of time, so give it a go and see what value you get. You may also want to consider forming your own but recognise that you will need to put in the necessary time and effort to get it off the ground.

→ **Benchmarking:** perhaps the most valuable way of identifying new ideas and stretching the way you think, but take a certain amount of effort to set up and manage. *Fast Track recommendation*: definitely worth doing, so identify two or three other organisations who you respect as being high performers, and meet them up to four times a year, making sure you use a facilitator and follow a structure agenda to maximise the cross-company learning. Remember that you will have to give value to them as well as the other way round.

→ **Professional bodies:** membership of these bodies becomes more important the more senior you become, and are often a source of free advice. *Fast Track recommendation*: once you have been in your role for at least a year, sign up for an initial trial period and see what benefits you receive.

→ **Fast-Track-Me.com:** all of the key ideas, tools and techniques contained in the Fast Track series are available via the internet at **www.Fast-Track-Me.com**. *Fast Track recommendation*: firstly, allocate 30 minutes to visit and explore the site. It contains a rich source of tips, tools and techniques, stories, expert voices and online audits from all of the Fast Track series.

Remember that whatever your source of information, to maximise the benefits you need to put time aside and make the necessary effort. However, also recognise that you will never have perfect knowledge. Take time to develop your skills in assessing the validity and reliability of the information you have, then decide what level of certainty will be good enough and act on it. Remember that as the figure below shows, seeking information and removing uncertainties becomes more expensive until, for example, the last 2 per cent is prohibitively expensive. The dangerous area in the middle highlights the risk of making important decisions on limited information.

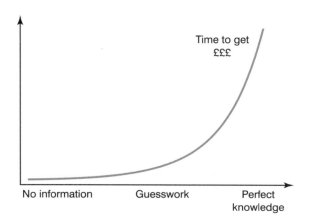

Getting promoted

At the appropriate time the Fast Track manager will seek promotion again. This may occur within a few months or possibly a number of years, but in either case take time to reflect on your state of readiness. Identify the future role you are keen to fulfil, clarify the criteria you will need to satisfy in terms of skills, experience, attitudes and behaviours, and consider how you will visibly demonstrate these attributes to others. Ask yourself, in relation to the following:

→ **Capability:** Do I have what it takes in terms of what I have achieved and learned so far?

→ **Credibility:** Can I convince others that I can and will perform the role well?

→ **Desire:** Do I want the role, and do I have sufficient drive and enthusiasm to do a great job?

→ **Relationships:** Do I have positive working relationships with the right people?

→ **Competitiveness:** Am I the most appropriate candidate, given the internal and external alternatives?

If you have concerns, then put in place a plan to address them. Timing will be key so make sure you are well prepared before putting yourself forward for the role. Learn how to package yourself by seeking advice and gaining feedback.

Becoming a director

 CASE STORY *LOCATION, LOCATION, LOCATION, HENRY'S STORY*

Narrator Henry was the managing director and shareholder in a distribution business.

Context While Henry owned 30 per cent of the company an entrepreneur owned the other 70 per cent. As well as this company, the entrepreneur's holding company also contained a wide portfolio of companies.

Issue Henry's business was located in the south-east of England while the entrepreneur and his main companies were in Edinburgh, Scotland. The entrepreneur decided that she wanted to bring Henry's distribution, particularly purchasing, knowledge on to the main board and offered him a position as executive director of the holding company. Henry was very pleased. He attended his first board meeting and realised that he knew little about the other businesses in the portfolio. He and the entrepreneur realised quite quickly that he could not really play a full part on the board of the holding company unless he spent a lot more time in Edinburgh.

Solution Henry was clearly faced with a choice – move or stay put and resign from the holding company board.

Learning Being an executive member of a board is a lot more than just attending board meetings. A director needs to be close to the main action of the company, listening to the water cooler conversations and meeting other directors and managers on a regular basis. They cannot just offer their expertise as though in a vacuum.

What are the statutory responsibilities of a director?

As well as heading up your function's activities throughout the business, you will have certain roles and statutory responsibilities that accompany the title of director. As a member of the board, you will be responsible to the shareholders of the company and be involved in:

→ determining the company's strategic objectives and policies

→ monitoring progress towards achieving the objectives and policies

→ appointing the senior management team

→ accounting for the company's activities to relevant parties (e.g. shareholders)

→ ensuring you meet regulatory requirements, environmental standards and corporate social responsibilities

→ attending board meetings that run the company, with the high level of integrity that is inferred by statutory standards and the company's interpretation of corporate governance, particularly in sensitive areas such as health and safety.

You will also have to conduct yourself in a highly professional manner:

→ A director must not put himself in a position where the interests of the company conflict with his personal interest or his duty to a third party.

→ A director must not make a personal profit out of her position as a director unless she is permitted to do so by the company.

→ A director must act bona fide in what he considers is in the interests of the company as a whole, and not for any other purpose and with no other agenda.

What is the role of the director?

Few organisations have the formal title of performance management director, but most will have a member of the executive team committed to driving team results forward. Here, managers will have a specific reference to performance management being a requirement of their role. Very often this will go further to state the process and system/documents to complete. Performance management is also added to the managers' objectives and their performance will be reviewed quarterly. These objectives are also aligned to salary increases or performance bonuses. In some organisations the HR Director or the Director of Operations will be responsible for performance management. Whatever the title, this senior manager will fulfil various roles in addition to meeting statutory responsibilities:

→ setting the overall performance management strategy and gaining the active support of the chief executive and other members of the board

→ championing performance management so that sufficient budget and resources are assigned to such activities, such as training, across the organisation in the face of competition from operating divisions and other functions

→ ensuring members of the board are aware of critical trends in the technology and the marketplace, the possible impact of each on business performance, and the implications in terms of driving fundamental change

→ designing the overall strategic framework and putting in place the appropriate teams and champions to ensure effective implementation

→ reporting on progress and performance to the board, conducting stakeholder presentations and briefing key opinion leaders inside and outside the organisation.

How do I get to the top?

Here is a summary and short personal test to find out what you need to do to get that chair in the boardroom. Starting with education, there are various business education programmes that will help to prepare you for becoming a company director. The Institute of Directors runs a full range of programmes for directors covering:

→ Being a director. This covers areas such as the responsibilities of being a company director, governance, administration, being a board member, dealing with the City.

→ Being a director in the context of a particular discipline (e.g. marketing, finance, risk, sales, operations).

The business schools also run similar programmes that you may consider. Make sure that you plan these programmes into your development plan so that you receive the training well before any future promotion and get support from your company to attend.

OK, so you've decided you need to confirm what you want in your life before taking on a director's role. Is it the right commitment for you to make? Now ask yourself if you have the bandwidth and skills to take on such a role. Does such a role suit your personality and values? Will you be able to live the other areas of your life the way that you want? In other words, does being a company director support the balance you may want to achieve in your life?

Create a life plan. Think of your life as a rocket. The rocket has fuel and rocket motors to give it the momentum to reach its objective. It has a vision, mission and guidance system (values) that guide the rocket on its way towards the vision. If you were NASA you would have a vision 'to charter the universes beyond our solar system in order to discover what alternative planets there are for habitation'. NASA's mission might be 'to build a colony on Mars by 2020 that enables the study of other universes'.

What is the aspiration or vision you have for your life?

Actions in your plan

Internal perspective

Make sure that you spend time with the senior people running the business to understand the overall **mechanics** of the business and how it works. **Network** with other people from similar businesses to get perspective on **future trends**.

Have views around the structure of the business and how it might need to change to meet goals and challenges.

External perspective

Look at the developments in the industry and think about what the future holds for the type of products and services the industry offers. How will changes in legislation affect the industry? How will technology impact the industry? How will changes in societal behaviours have an impact?

Sponsors for your career

Work on establishing a sponsor or a number of sponsors who are advocating your growth path and represent you in influential groups that you can't reach yourself. Your sponsor will be someone who is already on the board or is an influencer at board level.

Build the right stakeholder relationships

Build relationships with as many key stakeholders as you can at board level. These would be board directors and non-executive directors. Attend as many forums as you can where there is an opportunity to meet them and develop relationships. Make sure that you are present in strategic forums and that you demonstrate capability in this area.

Demonstrate an ability to model success

It's important to be able to demonstrate that you can recreate success through models for success that work. The easy way to demonstrate this is through the strategic frameworks that you establish and publish to your key stakeholders. Make sure that you make your successes known. Business leaders need to be able to model successful strategies for their followers.

Create win/win outcomes

What will be the pay-off for other directors when you are a member of their team? You need to build a reputation as someone who wants to ensure that others achieve their business and personal goals.

Your path to promotion will be much easier because people want you playing on the same field.

Personal development

Get hold of a competency framework for directors and do your own gap analysis to understand what skills are required to fulfil a director's role. Work with a coach to help you to close the gap.

Finally, develop your personal scorecard to prioritise the areas you need to work on developing.

AREA	SCORE OUT OF 10	PRIORITY AREA TO WORK ON
Understand internal perspective	7	
Understand external perspective	4	1
Sponsors for your career	3	2
Build the right stakeholder relationships	3	3
An ability to model success for others	8	
Create win/wins	7	
Personal development	8	

QUICK TIP FIND THE RIGHT MENTOR
Find a director who is willing to mentor you on how to fulfil the criteria for becoming a director through their own experience of having been through the process themselves.

Planning your 'exit strategy'

How long do you want to be in each job you do before moving on to your next promotion? Looked at logically it takes about ten weeks, as we have seen in Chapter 5, to take stock of the new job, set the new direction and start the process of implementing your strategy and plan. You probably need to give it a year to demonstrate its success; so after a year and ten weeks the time has come to sniff around for a new job.

This is why you need to plan an exit strategy. You want to be indispensable to the organisation but not to the job you are doing at the moment. You do not want to be the victim of senior people saying that they need you to stay put because you are getting good results in an area that is important to the organisation. Identify as quickly as you can at least one and preferably two people who you will groom to take over your job. In order to do this, always recruit the best people you can attract. It's much better to have someone who really wants your job than to play safe and recruit people who are just not as good as you.

So, work out your next step, make sure there is someone to step into your shoes and the organisational world is your ostrich!

 STOP – THINK – ACT

But before then, stop and reflect on your career aspirations – what do you want to be doing in three years' time?

My vision	What do I want to be doing in three years' time?
My supporters	Whose support will I need to get there?
My capabilities	What capabilities and experience will I need to succeed?
My progress	What milestones will I achieve along the way?

Visit **www.Fast-Track-Me.com** to use the Fast Track online planning tool.

The competencies method for assessing staff

Professor Victor Dulewicz, Henley Business School, University of Reading

EXPERT VOICE

Selecting the right people is crucial to the success of any organisation. To do this, you have to have a clear idea of the job requirements – the ability, aptitude, skills, personality and motivation of people to do the job – otherwise you don't know if you have hit your 'target'. The competencies approach is a proven method for doing this. It can also be used for training, development and appraisal applications and is nowadays at the heart of most large organisations' HR processes.

The competencies approach was first devised in the early 1970s by the US consultancy company, McBer, to identify those personal characteristics which result in effective and/or superior job performance. According to Professor Richard Boyatzis's book documenting the McBer work, 'a job competency is an underlying characteristic of a person in that it may be a motive, trait, skill, aspect of one's self-image or social role, or a body of knowledge which he or she uses'.[1] Competencies are usually identified using critical incident or repertory grid interviews or surveys and assessed by interviews, psychometric tests, assessment/development centres and questionnaires.

This approach is often referred to as personal competencies, as opposed to the occupational competencies or standards approach which concentrates on the job, as opposed to the individual, and aims to specify in very detailed behavioural terms standards of performance required to carry out a job competently or effectively. The standards approach has been used widely in the UK since the late 1980s as an assessment tool for accrediting National Vocational Qualifications (NVQs) for a wide range of jobs from semi-skilled up to middle-management levels. However, we will concentrate here on the personal competencies approach since it is much more appropriate to many HR processes.

A good example of a well-tested and proven personal competencies model is the personal competencies survey (PCS), which has been developed and refined by the author over the past 25 years through his work on management assessment and competencies. Its design drew heavily on the extant literature and has been widely used as a job analysis tool for identifying the competencies required by effective senior and middle

---

[1] Boyatzis, R. (2009) Special Issue on Competencies, *Journal of Management Development*, 28, 9, pp. 749–875.

managers in large companies such as Shell International, Barclays, British Gas and Smiths Group. It was also used for many years for appraisal on the senior management courses at Henley Management College, and has subsequently been used for other white-collar jobs below management levels. It has been constantly revised on the basis of evidence from extensive applications and research in many countries.

The overall framework is comprehensive, consisting of 45 competencies under six main headings covering intellectual, personal, communication, interpersonal, leadership and results-orientation competencies. The titles of the competencies are presented in the table opposite. Each one has a behavioural definition, e.g.:

25 **Oral Presentation:** In formal presentations, is concise and to the point; does not use jargon without explanation; tailors content to the audience's understanding. Is enthusiastic and lively when speaking.

32 **Planning:** Establishes future priorities and visualises all foreseeable changes required to meet future requirements. Identifies appropriate resource requirements, including staff, to achieve long-term objectives.

Details of the Personal Competencies Survey (PCS) are available from Dulewicz.[2] This model is fairly typical of the generic competency frameworks currently used in the UK.

Those needing to identify the competencies required for successful performance, for personnel selection, development or appraisal schemes, are advised to use existing competencies questionnaires such as the PCs or to develop tailored versions using the framework in the table opposite as a starting point, and then writing their own definitions of the behaviours which constitute high performance. They can validate this by comparing the ratings of high and low performers and then identifying those competencies which produce significant differences between the two groups. Those which differentiate constitute the profile of high performers in a specific job in your organisation, which can then be incorporated into your personnel selection, development or appraisal schemes.

[2] Dulewicz, V. (2010) Personal Competencies Survey. **www.dulewicz.com**

PERSONAL COMPETENCIES FRAMEWORK

I: Intellectual	IV: Inter-personal
1 Information collection	26 Impact
2 Problem analysis	27 Persuasiveness
3 Numerical interpretation	28 Sensitivity
4 Judgement	29 Flexibility
5 Critical faculty	30 Ascendancy
6 Creativity	31 Negotiating
7 Planning	
8 Perspective	
9 Organisational awareness	
10 External awareness	
11 Learning-oriented	
12 Technical expertise	
II: Personal	**V: Leadership**
13 Adaptability	32 Organising
14 Independence	33 Empowering
15 Integrity	34 Appraising
16 Stress tolerance	35 Motivating others
17 Resilience	36 Developing others
18 Detail consciousness	37 Leading
19 Self-management	
20 Change-oriented	
III: Communication	**VI: Results-orientation**
21 Reading	38 Risk taking
22 Written communication	39 Decisiveness
23 Listening	40 Business sense
24 Oral expression	41 Energy
25 Oral presentation	42 Concern for excellence
	43 Tenacity
	44 Initiative
	45 Customer-oriented

EXPERT VOICE

PART D

DIRECTOR'S
TOOLKIT

In Part B we introduced ten core tools and techniques that can be used from day one in your new role as a team leader or manager in your chosen field. As you progress up the career ladder to the role of senior manager, and as your team matures in terms of its understanding and capabilities, you will want to introduce more advanced and sophisticated techniques.

Part D provides a number of more advanced techniques[1] developed and adopted by industry leaders – helping you to stand out from your competitors.

	TOOL DESCRIPTION
T1	Performance audit
T2	Team audit
T3	Talent passport

---

[1] All tools and techniques are available online at **www.Fast-Track-Me.com**

T1 PERFORMANCE AUDIT

Use the following checklist to assess the current state of your team. Consider each criterion in turn and use the following scoring system to identify current performance:

0 Not done or defined within the team: unaware of its importance to performance management

1 Aware of area but little or no work done in the team

2 Recognised as an area of importance and some work done in this area

3 Area clearly defined and work done in the area in terms of performance management

4 Consistent use of best practice tools and techniques in this area across the team

5 Area is recognised as being 'best in class' and could be a reference area for best practice.

Then reflect on the lowest scores and identify those areas that are critical to success and flag them as status Red requiring immediate attention. Then identify those areas that you are concerned about, and flag those as status Amber, implying areas of risk that need to be monitored closely. Status Green implies that you are happy with the current state.

ID	CATEGORY	EVALUATION CRITERIA	SCORE	STATUS
1	**Vision**		0–5	RAG
A	Clear vision	The team has a clear vision and mission for the future looking out at least three years		
B	Strategic framework	The team has translated that vision into a tangible strategy that defines what products and services it will provide and the internal and external customers that it will serve		
C	Business goals	The team also understands what the current business and team goals are for this reporting period, and what their relative priority is		
2	**Business DNA**			
A	Key performance indicators	The team has a defined set of KPIs that are SMART: specific to the team, measurable, achievable, relevant and time-bound		
B	Balanced scorecard	The KPIs are balanced in terms of being backward and forward (predictive) looking, and in terms of financial results focus and non-financial focus (team brand, operational effectiveness and team development)		
C	Clear ownership	Each KPI has an owner within the team that is responsible for performance		
3	**High-performance teams**			
A	Optimum structure	The team is structured to reflect the core processes of the team and the core roles being performed		
B	Team plans	There is a plan for the continuous improvement of team performance based on the principles of a 'high performance team'		
C	Balanced composition	The team is balanced in terms of skills, experience, diversity and levels of the team members		
4	**'A' players**			
A	Key contributors	Whilst the contribution of everyone is recognised, the key contributors towards high performance have been identified		
B	Leadership development	There is a leadership and skills development programme for all 'A' players that maximises their contribution to overall team performance		
C	Talent management	There is a broader talent management programme that continuously develops the skills across all team members		

ID	CATEGORY	EVALUATION CRITERIA	SCORE	STATUS
5	**Business continuity**		0–5	RAG
A	Key role identification	The key roles in the team have been identified – those individuals that will ultimately be responsible for delivery against team goals		
B	Succession planning	There are succession plans for all key roles that reduce the possibility of gaps and reduce dependency on key individuals		
C	Risk management	All team risks have been identified and captured on a risk register that also states agreed mitigation actions, ownership and timing		
6	**Motivating change**			
A	Continuous innovation	There is a programme of innovation where creative ideas for performance improvement are fed into a team forum for review		
B	Involvement of all teams	All members of the team are actively engaged in the innovation programme and act as the 'eyes and ears' of the team		
C	High level of motivation	All members of the team are highly motivated to generate ideas for improvement, and successes are recognised and rewarded		
7	**Developing people**			
A	Personal profiles	All members of the team have their own personal profiles that capture their current skills and competencies and their previous experience		
B	Personal development plans (PDPs)	Everyone in the team has regular plans for improving specific skills in line with their needs and the needs of the team		
C	Knowledge management	There is a forum where lessons learned and new insights are captured, assessed and shared amongst the team		
8	**Right behaviours/right attitudes**			
A	Organisational culture	The overall values and beliefs of the team support high performance, reinforced by effective systems, processes and routines		
B	Right behaviours	All members of the team exhibit the right behaviours in support of the overall goals and the team culture		
C	Right attitudes	All members of the team have a positive attitude towards performance improvement		

ID	CATEGORY	EVALUATION CRITERIA	SCORE	STATUS
9	**Effective governance**		0–5	RAG
A	Compliance	The team is compliant with all internal and external rules, standards and laws		
B	Best practice	The team continuously evaluates best-in-class companies and implement best practice in order to improve performance		
C	Performance reviews	The leader conducts regular (no more than monthly) reviews of progress towards goals and performance against KPIs		
10	**Gaining visibility**			
A	Performance dashboards	There is a performance dashboard that reflects the 1:3:10 rule for all KPIs. Within 1 second the team knows whether the KPI is on or off track, within 3 seconds it knows the trend, and within 10 seconds it can tell what the cause is and what action is being taken		
B	Anywhere, anytime access	The dashboard is captured and presented within a web-based system that allows all key stakeholder anywhere, anytime access to real-time performance data		
C	Focus on actions	The performance dashboard focus reviews on the areas of concern (Red and Amber indicators) and on actions that have clear ownership and timing		

For each element of the checklist add up the scores of the three related questions and divide by 3 – this will give you an average score for that specific element: see the example below.

ELEMENT	SCORE	0	1	2	3	4	5	NOTES
Vision	2.1			■				Strategy has notbeen communicated effectively
Business DNA	4.2					■		
High-performance teams	3.6				■			The key roles are not defined
'A' players	4.6						■	
Business continuity	1.7		■					No succession planning
Motivating change	2.6			■				High resistance to change
Developing people	1.2		■					No personal development plans in place
Right behaviours/ attitudes	4.6						■	
Effective governance	4.4					■		
Gain visibility	3.8					■		Dashboard still Excel-based

In your performance framework the whole performance management process is only as good as each individual element. If one 'link in the chain' is weak, then the performance process within the company will not operate to optimum efficiency and there is an increased risk of failure. The action plan therefore should be to focus attention and resources on the elements of greatest weakness first, and then to move the whole framework to a level of excellence. This approach optimises the use of resources and sets up a process of continuous improvement.

In the example opposite, the managers conducting the performance audit have identified that the weakest link is that of *Developing people* (average score 1.2). The plan would therefore be to focus attention on and improve this area first until it was no longer the weakest link. Once the senior management team has increased confidence that this area has improved, the next stage would be to focus on *Business continuity* (1.7) and *Vision* (2.1) areas.

Visit **www.Fast-Track-Me.com** to complete this diagnostic online, and capture actions for performance improvement.

T2 TEAM AUDIT

Use the following template to assess the current maturity of your team. Start by confirming the team purpose and strategy, and then use the team audit checklist questions to assess your current state. Use the guidance notes at the end of the template as you progress – this will help you interpret the example and to apply the techniques to your own team.

Team profile

	REFERENCE
Reference	CCSE – S&M
Team name	Marketing team
Purpose	Sales and marketing function for Sweden and the Nordic countries
Team leader	Ross (David)
Executive sponsor	Bruce (Andy)

	SCOPE	TEAM PLAN
A	Vision	To establish our brand as the leading product in our strategic markets – the 'preferred supplier'
B	Mission	To increase turnover by 50 per cent and gain market leadership over a three-year period
C	Values	We seek to aggressively dominate our target markets whilst working collaboratively with our strategic partners. We will work with clients to improve their overall return-on-investment in our solutions
D	Strategic priorities	In order to deliver against the vision and goals, the following areas need to be addressed: (1) an international scanning system, (2) greater automation of the field sales force, (3) closer alignment with strategic partners, and (4) greater investment in brand
E	Short-term goal	Realign sales towards current strategic targets, and improve overall profitability through reduced costs associated with customer tail 'complexity'
F	Medium-term goal	Establish our business as the major player in the Nordic region as well as expanding through strategic partners in other European states
G	Long-term goal	Gain overall market leadership across Europe and seek to consolidate the competition either through acquisition or through market forces

Team audit

	1. OVERRIDING SENSE OF PURPOSE	SCORE	NOTES
A	Shares commitments	4	
B	Has a clear business purpose	5	
C	Has a strategy and shared vision	4	
D	Commits to achieving high standards	4	
E	Delivers measurable results	5	
	2. BUILDS ON STRENGTHS AND SKILLS	SCORE	NOTES
A	Shares leadership	1	
B	Recognises, encourages and employs team members' technical competencies	1	
C	Has an accountable leader who ensures the team has what is necessary to do the job	1	
D	Develops team members' competencies to meet goals	1	

3. STRONG RESULTS ETHIC	SCORE	NOTES
A	Discloses hidden agendas	4	
B	Shares knowledge, skills and feelings	0	
C	Focuses on the issue	1	
D	Seeks to leverage conflict	1	
E	Ensures active communication with stakeholders	2	
F	Creates a safe environment, enabling team members to speak up on issues	2	
G	Establishes and uses roles and norms	1	

4. OPEN COMMUNICATIONS AND MUTUAL ACCOUNTABILITY	SCORE	NOTES
A	Establishes clear targets and measures	5	
B	Applies effective processes to achieve goals	4	
C	Works beyond expectations	4	
D	Holds a shared passion for success	4	
E	Integrates its team members	5	
F	Balances drive and empathy	4	
G	Actively works to establish effective task, process and climate	5	
H	Celebrates achievement	3	
I	Works through adversity	5	
J	Strives for creative solutions	4	
K	Makes decisions effectively	5	

5. COHESIVE, COMPASSIONATE AND UNIFIED TEAM	SCORE	NOTES
A	Displays no obvious hierarchy	4	
B	Commits to and works on becoming better	2	
C	Coordinates activities	2	
D	Defines and aligns key processes (meetings, planning, decision making, feedback)	5	
E	Shares and takes considered risks	0	
F	Seeks support from and offers it to wide company	1	
G	Shows concern for team members' well-being	2	
H	Defines members' agreed contribution	4	
I	Has members who volunteer support in meeting team needs	5	

6. UNIQUE SOCIAL SYSTEM	SCORE	NOTES
A	Actively encourages and benefits from diversity	4	
B	Members perceive they know, trust and respect each other	4	
C	Balances organisational, team and individual social needs	4	
D	Members enjoy working and playing together	3	

Team audit summary

		CHARACTERISTICS OF HIGH-PERFORMING TEAMS	PERCENTAGE IDEAL	STATUS
1	PURPOSE	Overriding sense of purpose	88	3-Green
2	STRENGTHS	Builds on strengths and skills	20	1-Red
3	RESULTS	Strong results ethic	31	1-Red
4	COMMUNICATIONS	Open communications and mutual accountability	87	3-Green
5	UNIFIED	Cohesive, compassionate and unified team	56	2-Amber
6	SOCIAL	Unique social system	75	3-Green
		SUMMARY	60	1-Red

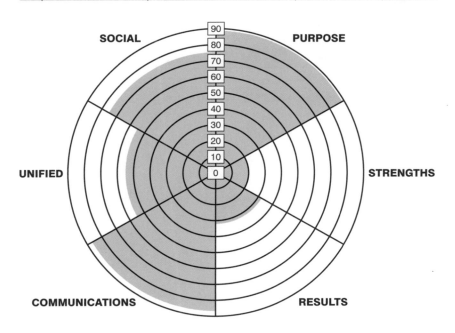

In the above figure, the team leader has three areas of concern that need to be addressed in the following order of priority:

1 The team does not build on the strengths and skills of team members.

2 The team does not have a strong results ethic.

3 It is not yet a cohesive, compassionate and unified team.

To identify and agree the actions necessary to improve performance, review the individual scores within each section of the team audit.

GUIDANCE NOTES

Use the following guidance notes to complete an initial audit of your team.

Reference

What is the unique identification given to this Team Audit?
Note: the ID, title, description and owner will all be entered and updated in the reference form.

Team name

What is the brief name given to this team?

Purpose

What is the primary purpose for this team?

Team leader

Who is the manager or leader for this team?

Executive sponsor

Which member of the senior management team is responsible for the business performance delivered by this team?

Review stage

How advanced is this review?

Last review

When was the performance and structure of this team last reviewed?

Next review

What date is the next audit planned for?

Documents

What attached documents are associated with this team or review?

Improvement projects

What are the projects and activities being undertaken to improve the performance of this team?

TEAM PROFILE

Vision

What is the overall vision for the team? Think ahead 3–5 years and identify what success will look like.

Mission

What is the specific mission for the team? Reflect on the purpose of the team and the overall mission, and identify one overriding target for this team?

Pillars

What are the fundamental building blocks or key success factors for this team?

Goals

What are the specific goals to be achieved?

Key economic indicator

What is the one key economic indicator that can be measured to indicate financial performance?

TEAM AUDIT

Evaluation criteria

What criteria are used to assess performance of this team?

SCORE

Use a simple five-point scale where:

1 = No visible awareness of the team characteristic
2 = Shows awareness of the characteristic but is not proficient
3 = Demonstrates the characteristic but only under strong leadership
4 = Demonstrates the characteristic without the need for supervision
5 = Best practice and would be used as a reference for other teams.

T3 TALENT PASSPORT

Use the following template to track the progress and performance of the key members of your team. Use the guidance notes at the end of the templates as you progress.

Talent tracker

		SUMMARY		STATUS
A	Position ID	SM.034	Stage	First 100 days
B	Job title	Sales and Marketing Manager	Function	Sales & Marketing
C	Role description	S&M Director for the sale of branded products into European markets	Availability	2009-Q4
D	Person	Bruce (Andy)	Next role	Sales Director
E	Manager	Edwards (Mark)	Performance	10
F	Coach	Ross (David)	Potential	35
G	Team	EMEA	Status	1-Red

Performance

	METRIC	DESCRIPTION	EVIDENCE	PERCENTAGE TARGET	STATUS	PDPs
A	Revenue growth	Increase top line sales by 5% in the current financial year		20	2-Amber	0
B	Profitability	Increase average gross contribution to 15% across all SKUs		10	2-Amber	0
C	Complexity reduction	Reduction of customer and product tail to lower overhead costs		30	1-Red	0
D	Strategic repositioning	Realignment of sales with strategic product-market priorities		20	1-Red	1

Potential

	METRIC	DESCRIPTION	EVIDENCE	LEVEL	STATUS	PDPs
A	Learning agility	Willingness to constantly challenge the status quo and drive through required changes		100	3-Green	0
B	Drive	Self-motivated to work towards KPIs with no supervision or reviews		40	1-Red	0
C	Innovation	High level of flexibility and positive approach to continuous innovation and improvement		70	3-Green	0
D	Judgement	Effective decision maker, balancing rational and creative criteria		90	3-Green	0

Rocketship

	SCOPE	PERSONAL STRATEGIC FRAMEWORK
A	Vision	
B	Mission	
C	Values	
D	Strategic priorities	
E	Short-term goal	
F	Medium-term goal	
G	Long-term goal	

Way-of-being

	Developed behaviours	0–7 YEARS	8–14 YEARS	15–21 YEARS
		ENABLING		
+ve	Collaboration			
+ve	Building a team			
+ve	Leadership			
		RESTRICTING		
–ve	Collaboration			
–ve	Building a team			
–ve	Leadership			

Personality filters

	DIMENSIONS	SCORE	DIMENSIONS	IMPLICATIONS
D1	Big chunk	-3	Small chunk	
D2	Necessity	2	Possibility	
D3	Similarity	2	Difference	
D4	Away from	4	Towards	
D5	Internal ref	3	External ref	
D6	Self	-2	Other	
D7	Associated	2	Disassociated	

Personal CV

	COMPETENCY	PROFILE AND EVIDENCE	POTENTIAL RATING	CURRENT RATING	STATUS	PDPS
	COMPETENCY					
L1	Value creation	Andy has consistently been the top sales person for the UK operation over a five-year period – defining and driving the re-engineering solution	4	4	3-Green	0
L2	Customer orientation	He is comfortable making exective presentations at a senior level but needs to get more involved in executive networking events	5	3	2-Amber	0
L3	Achieving excellence	He is a perfectionist and always seeks to improve on how things are done – based on a good understanding of latest market trends	3	4	3-Green	0
L4	Developing others	He could spend more time coaching – something he is good at	5	3	2-Amber	0
L5	Business awareness	He has an MBA and a strong business acumen. He has also developed the external business accelerator programme	5	4	3-Green	0
L6	Collaboration and teamwork	Whilst comfortable working alone, he is a strong contributor to the team and enjoys working on team challenges with others	2	3	3-Green	0

			POTENTIAL	CURRENT RATING	STATUS	PDPS
L7	Innovation and change management	Andy continually challenges the status quo and seeks to identify tangible actions to improve the way things are done	5	5	3-Green	0
L8	Leadership	He is comfortable leading, but could invest more time really making sure others have his vision and clarity of direction	4	3	2-Amber	0
					2-Amber	

EXPERIENCE		DESCRIPTION	POTENTIAL	CURRENT RATING	STATUS	PDPS
E1	Previous roles	International sales manager; field technical sales support, marketing manager	A	B	3-Green	0
E2	Project involvement	Conferences, Six Sigma, CI programme	B	C	2-Amber	0
E3	Academic qualifications	MBA; BSc Mech Eng; SofTools Programme Leader	A	A	3-Green	0
E4	Professional and memberships	None	B	D	1-Red	0
					1-Red	

Guidance notes

Now use the following guidance notes to complete an initial audit of your team.

Talent tracker

Position ID What is the unique reference for this role? (*Note*: this reference will start with an R if specific to the Role, and P if specific to the Person.)

Job title What is the formal job title for this role?

Role description What is the full description of this role?

Person Who the person fulfilling this role?

Manager Who is the manager for this person?

Coach Who is the coach for this manager?

Team Which division or team does this person belong to?

Stage What stage role maturity applies?

Function What function does this role relate to?

Availability In what period is this person likely to be ready or available for promotion?

Next role What is their next role likely to be?

Performance What level of current performance have you achieved?

Note: Scores for both performance and potential will be delivered from the following forms.

Potential What is your potential performance level?

Status What is the current status for this person in this role? This will be the worst-case scenario of actual performance and actual competence, and will be calculated automatically by the system.

Performance

KPI What are the key performance indicators for this role?

KPI measure and target performance What is the measure of performance, and what is the target level of performance?

Current performance What is the current level of performance achieved by this person?

Rating What is the percentage of the ideal being achieved by this person? 0% = has never achieved the target performance.
20% = has rarely achieved target performance.
40% = achieves target performance some of the time but frequently underachieves.
60% = achieves target performance most of the time.
80% = achieves target performance consistently.
100% = consistently achieves better than expected performance.

Status What is the current performance (output) status for this role?
Red = Unsatisfactory and major concerns requiring immediate corrective action.
Amber = Satisfactory performance but some concerns and risks, and needs to be monitored closely.
Green = Satisfactory performance.

Potential

KPI What are the key performance indicators for this role?

KPI measure and target performance What is the measure of performance, and what is the target level of performance?

Current performance What is the current level of performance achieved by this person?

Rating What is the percentage of the ideal being achieved by this person? 0% = has never achieved the target performance.
20% = has rarely achieved target performance.
40% = achieves target performance some of the time but frequently underachieves.

60% = achieves target performance most of the time.

80% = achieves target performance consistently.

100% = consistently achieves better than expected performance.

Status What is the current performance (output) status for this role?
Red = Unsatisfactory and major concerns requiring immediate corrective action.
Amber = Satisfactory performance but some concerns and risks, and needs to be monitored closely.
Green = Satisfactory performance.

Rocketship

Vision What is your vision of the future? Bring this vision to fruition by describing in great detail what you will be doing and how you will be doing it.

Mission What is your overall mission or purpose? Think about what you will have achieved by the end of your career.

Values What values will guide your decision making or restrict the choices you have?

Pillars What are the fundamental building blocks or pillars that will enable you to achieve your vision?

Goals What are your short-, medium- and long-term goals that will enable you to move towards your vision? Short = this 12 month period. Medium = 2–3 years. Long = beyond three years.

Way-of-being

Developed behaviours What behaviours have been developed in each of three key development phases of your life? 0–7 years old, 8–14 years old and 15–21 years old.

Impact on performance How does each developed behaviour enable or restrict your ability to form in three key dimensions: collaboration, building a team, leadership?

Personality filters

Dimensions What dimensions will be used to assess a person's ability and willingness to change?

Implications What evidence or proof is there of a person's ability and willingness to change?

Status What is the current status against each dimension?

PDPs What personal development plans have you initiated in order to address Red and Amber status dimensions?

Definitions
We completed the elicitation of your personality filters, which are like pairs of spectacles you habitually wear, letting in only a certain amount or type of light. These personality filters are one of the mechanisms through which you delete, distort and generalise information coming to you.

Big chunk vs small chunk
This is about whether you tend to focus on the big picture or the detail, and to establish this please could you talk through how you would go about setting up a project.

Big chunk – strategic thinker, sees connections between things, the big picture, can deal with ambiguity.

Small chunk – nitty gritty details. Likes certainty, structure, processes.

Necessity vs possibility
This is about why you choose to do what you are doing. If I asked you why you run, in reply you could give a number of reasons, indicating you have a choice and purpose in your running. If you had no reasons for doing it, that would be an indication that you were operating out of necessity.

Necessity – needs structure to operate in, should, ought, must, have to, need to, got to.

Possibility – thrives on choices, options, possibility, could, can, see what happens, may be spontaneity.

Similarity vs difference

This is about the relationship between things, events, people, etc. I could ask you to tell me about three coins (5p pieces) I put on the table. You may talk about the similarities or talk about the differences. You could also talk about both in the same measure.

> *Similarity* – wants the status quo, notices how things are alike, doesn't like change. Not wonderful on analysis

> *Difference* – likes change, new ideas, innovation, good on analysis

Away from vs towards

This is about direction – whether you are moving away from/avoiding something, or whether you are moving towards. If I were to ask you what is important to you about holidays or your car, for example, I would note whether you would describe what you did want or what you didn't want.

> *Away from* – careful, risk averse, know what they don't want, has consequences in mind

> *Towards* – know what they want, thinks goals and not consequences

Internal reference vs external reference

This is about where you get your feedback from, whether it is self-generated and you just know how you are doing, or whether you need external verification from people or from data.

> *Internal reference* – likes own counsel. I think, I want, I feel

> *External reference* – seeks re-enforcement from outside sources, consensus agreement, to be recognised by others

Self vs other

This is about where your attention is directed – to yourself or to others.

> *Self* – high on 'do as I do', leads by example, I, me, selfish

> *Others* – concerned how others will respond, guided by others' opinions or needs

Associated vs disassociated

> *Associated* – is in time

> *Disassociated* – reflective, ability to stand back

Curriculum vitae

Competencies What core competencies does this require for success?

Leadership What are the core leadership competencies?

Experience What experience has this person had?

Roles What are the last three roles fulfilled?

Projects What project and change management experience does the person have?

Qualifications What formal academic qualifications does the person have?

Professional What memberships of professional bodies are held?

Traits What is the personality profile of the person?

Description What is the fuller description of each competency?

Target rating What is the target rating for ideal performance of the overall role? *Note*: expert coaching is not required in all areas!

Current rating What is the current rating of this person?

Status What is the current status for each item? Red = Major concerns (competency gaps) and immediate corrective action is required. Amber = Some concerns and risks, and needs to be monitored carefully to assess the impact on overall performance. Green = Satisfactory performance

PDPs How will the person develop Red and Amber areas of competency?

Skills

What is the current skillset, and what are the desired future skills to acquire for the current or future role?

Career drivers

Drivers What are the things that excite you at work that will influence the type of work or career you will want do follow in the future?

Dislikes What are the things you dislike at work that will influence what you will *not* want to do in the future? These will restrict future options you will take.

Responsibility What level of authority or responsibility do you seek? Some people enjoy working in technical roles on their own, whereas others seek to lead and manage.

Location Where (physically) do you want to work? This might reflect a preference for international travel or a desire to stay in a particular location.

Terms What terms and conditions influence your choice? Some people prefer a risk-free package where remuneration is guaranteed up front, whereas others would rather take a lower basic salary but with the potential to earn significant commission.

THE FAST TRACK WAY

Take time to reflect

Within the Fast Track series, we cover a lot of ground quickly. Depending on your current role, company or situation, some ideas will be more relevant than others. Go back to your individual and team audits and reflect on the 'gaps' you have identified, and then take time to review each of the top ten tools and techniques and list of technologies.

Next steps

Based on this review, you will identify many ideas about how to improve your performance, but look before you leap: take time to plan your next steps carefully. Rushing into action is rarely the best way to progress unless you are facing a crisis. Think carefully about your own personal career development and that of your team. Identify a starting place and consider what would have a significant impact on performance and be easy to implement. Then make a simple to-do list with timings for completion.

Staying ahead

Finally, the fact that you have taken time to read and think hard about the ideas presented here suggests that you are already a professional in your chosen discipline. However, all areas of business leadership are changing rapidly and you need to take steps to stay ahead as a leader in your field.

Take time to log in to the Fast Track web-resource, at **www.Fast-Track-Me.com**, and join a community of like-minded professionals.

Good Luck!

OTHER TITLES IN THE FAST TRACK SERIES

This title is one of many in the Fast Track series that you may be interested in exploring. Whilst each title works as a standalone solution, together they provide a comprehensive cross-functional approach that creates a common business language and structure. The series includes titles on the following:

- → Finance
- → Innovation
- → Strategy
- → Sales

- → Marketing
- → Project Management
- → Managing
- → Risk Management

GLOSSARY

'A' player An 'A' player is someone who exceeds expectations in 50 per cent or more of the skills required to do the role

Ansoff matrix A strategic diagram of product and market segments which illustrates, among other things, areas for growth, maintenance and decline in the future business

'B' player 'B' player is one who is good to very good in 50 per cent or more of the skills required to do the role

balanced scorecard A tool used to track progress against a series of pre-set business measures or key performance indicators (often strategic). 'Balanced' because it uses metrics relating to people development, operations and strategy as well as finance. Can be further enhanced to see performance of the whole team or even business on a single page

benchmark An approach to comparing performance (process, project, team or individual) with what is considered standard best practice. Benchmarking is driven by metrics such as cost, cycle time, productivity, or quality

budget The amount of resource available to support delivery of a goal. Budget can be measured in financial or human resource terms

budgeting The art or science of managing resource in a proactive manner such that shortfalls can be avoided or mitigated and sequencing of budget spend is matched to the rate at which budget is released

'C' player A 'C' player is below the level of a 'B' player and is someone who is good/average in 50 per cent or more of the skills. The role of a 'C' player is to support 'B' players. You would not have a 'C' player in leadership roles in your high-performing team

career path A journey from initial pay-check to retirement which is managed by systematic means to reach a certain goal or position. As opposed to the reactive work–life journey which reflects the ebb and flow of other people's decision making

cash cow A significant revenue generator in a non-growth segment whose profits are either distributed externally or internally to support growth in other areas (e.g. *The Sun* newspaper is a cash cow that enables News International to invest in digital news media)

change The process of evolution which underpins the continued profitability of any enterprise; if a business stands still, either its customers will move on or its competitors will move in. No change ultimately means a fall in volumes and margins

cloud This is a generic term for the new, virtual, externally hosted/provided/managed services that seamlessly integrate

coaching The use of (external) support to help a person develop full potential. Generally applied when a person is promoted to a new, more demanding position. It can also be a remedial step to kick-start a change in behaviour

consultants Typically an external thought-leadership resource who will challenge ways of thinking and help the senior management team to develop new strategies and aligned implementation plans. A consultant should not be viewed as a 'pair of hands' – brought in to alleviate workload or manage through a period of change

continuous improvement Ongoing efforts to improve products, services or processes to deliver incremental improvement over time. Typically a cycle of plan, do, check, act

contractors Hopefully inexpensive but experienced resource who can fill a short-term gap to enable delivery of a project. Ideally these people are not used within processes as they can become an expensive fixture. The beauty of contractors is that they usually have more flexible conditions – but beware as employment law is regularly changing

corporate coolade A liquid version of a corporate mind-washing mantra. Drinking this stuff is potentially dangerous and can seriously impair your ability to think as an individual (commonsense and sense of humour will start to wane)

cross-functional A key characteristic of any truly effective project or corporate initiative is that it is designed by multiple functions with a clear understanding of the benefits and issues which each function will experience as part of the project

CxO Chief Executive Officer and others like Chief Financial and Chief Operational Officer etc. Generic business term

CyO Future Generation Y CxOs

decision rights The restrictive framework within which you are allowed to operate and make decisions – e.g. budgets or hiring decisions may go beyond your decision rights. Set decision rights so people know their limits and to clarify expectations

delegation Getting other people to deliver because that is the best use of their time and enables you to make best use of yours

deliverables Where the rubber hits the road – tangible pieces of work that add value by themselves or pave the way for strategic and operational success

ERP Enterprise resource planning is normally a software system (series of applications) designed to integrate all the information and functions of a business or company from shared data stores

(corporate) ethics The basic beliefs of the organisation or team which guide actions and decisions – Fair Trade is a good example as it ethically drives all sourcing activity

executive summary A one-page overview of a situation setting out all the key aspects and developments associated with a particular business issue. A useful tool for securing buy-in from people who will do not have time or who will be switched off by reading a wordy presentation or report

exit interview A meeting held with a departing employee to establish the rationale for their departure; rarely done effectively, these are a tremendous opportunity to learn lessons to avoid potentially losing other good people

feedback The breakfast of champions! Feedback is a vital tool to secure input on what is being done well or badly. It should be designed/given in such a way that it sustains good performance or changes poor performance

FTE Full time employee – a person who is part of team headcount. FTEs are unlike contractors in that they are a relatively fixed overhead. This means they can be counted on if you need their time to work on a task but they cannot be switched off like a tap to reduce costs if times are tight

function and silos A team or department within an organisation that is responsible for delivering the outputs associated with a certain aspect of the business (e.g. IT,

Sales, Marketing). Some functions can be run as independent units with little interaction with other functions and are regarded as working in silos

Gantt chart A graphical representation of the sequencing of deliverables of a project over time (developed by Henry L Gantt during WW1 to help schedule the shipping of munitions from the USA to the EU to support the war effort)

gap analysis An understanding of the different levels of performance between where a team/function is versus where it needs to be. Typically a gap analysis may also include some form of recommendation on the work required to bridge the gap

HR Human Resources – a function that delivers increasing value along a spectrum from organising simple, routine tasks (e.g. sick pay, holidays and car policy) to driving the human and intellectual capital of the organisation – articulating stretching new strategies and building people's capacity to deliver

impact A noticeable difference – ideally positive and achieved as a result of planned actions

KPIs Key performance indicators – the standout metrics looked at to confirm good or bad performance. These can be either for the business as a whole (e.g. BSkyB is driven by ARPU – average revenue per user) or for specific functions or processes, such as productivity of a manufacturing line or performance vs sales targets

management levels The hierarchy of an organisation is sometimes formally divided into set management levels, and promotion is viewed not in terms of function or responsibility but in terms of progression from one level to another. Such systems tend to be less common as they are seen as

restricting entrepreneurial egalitarian thinking – they are typically still to be found in large denationalised businesses and quite regularly in big corporate businesses in the EU (especially Germany)

MBA Master of Business Administration – a qualification (usually seen as a second degree) based on giving students an insight into the theories and practices of management across a range of disciplines such as finance, marketing, human resources, operations and process design, etc. The objective of an MBA is to make the student a more rounded business professional – able to understand the drivers and issues of each business area and therefore able to move into management positions in different parts of a business

mentor An experienced (usually internal) senior manager who acts as a guide to newer, less experienced managers – challenging their thinking and helping them to become more mature, successful managers

mesh To instantly integrate

milestones Intermediate measures of success – staging posts on the way to successful delivery of a project. Milestones can be ad hoc to check progress (e.g. 'Where are we guys?' is a good question to ask after three months of frantic action) or planned (e.g. where will we be by Christmas; the annual sales conference could be a milestone during the roll-out of a new CRM platform)

morals Your personal sense of right and wrong. Not formally an integral part of a management structure but if your morals are questionable (non-existent) developing consistent loyalty may be tough

network All the people you have ever met – no matter how fleetingly. Your network may be more aware of you than you are of them

networking Getting out from behind your desk and meeting people – inside and outside the organisation

NPD New product development

operations The day-to-day running of the business and its functions

opportunity cost Doing anything within a work context costs time and resource; using time and resource for a new opportunity means that another aspect of the business will be starved of that resource. Will the new project offer a higher return on investment or will the cost of this new opportunity outweigh the benefits that could have been reaped by focusing elsewhere?

organisation structure – flat An organisation structure with only a few, often (deliberately) ill-defined levels – designed to encourage fluidity of information exchange and decision making

organisation structure – hierarchical An organisation structure with multiple, clearly defined and consistently articulated levels – designed to bring formality, consistency and rigour to information exchange and decision making

organisation structure – matrix An organisation structure (flat or hierarchical) where an employee will typically have more than one boss and set of objectives – often designed to ensure that, for example, functional and geographic goals are both addressed by the same person. Important that goals set by each boss are not conflicting!

ownership The intellectual claim over a key element of business strategy; the operational responsibility for a specific deliverable within the business (e.g. task, process, project)

pay scales Levels of pay – often associated with or determined by the management level at which an employee is working

PCS Personal competencies survey

PDP Personal development plan

performance management Managing (and rewarding) people or functions according to quality of output – not just by attendance

performance system A person's working environment which can often have an influence on the ability or desire to do a good job

portfolio management Managing a range of events, projects or tasks according to a set of common criteria in order to help prioritise and monitor progress of more than one aspect of business performance

process A repeating sequence of actions designed to deliver a specific output. Given its repeat nature, a process can typically be measured according to efficiency (output per consumed resource)

product market matrix A matrix – with product (existing, evolving, new) on the y-axis and markets (existing, evolving, new) on the x-axis – that enables a business to understand which services are delivered to which markets. Can be used to determine future direction/strategic opportunities

project A relatively complex (one-off) initiative or series of actions designed to deliver a specific tangible output – typically time-bound and with a known resource allocation

project management A structured approach to coordinating the deliverables of a project to ensure maximum value creation to meet the (ongoing) needs of key stakeholders

promotion An upward move within the corporate management structure. Regular promotion is regarded by many as the key indicator of career progression

recruitment Bringing new people into the team either to provide additional resource to handle a greater workload or to help to develop new strategies and fresh ways of working as a means of accelerating the journey towards strategic success

retention Keeping a winning team together by retaining key players is a key management skill. Main tools are tailored reward and recognition programmes as well as a clearly mapped career pathway for your top performers (which recognises that they will move on at some stage but ideally when you are prepared)

reward (management by) A token of recognition – a reward is only a reward if it is seen as such by the recipient. A manager's preference (e.g. tickets to the big game) – no matter how expensive – may not be received as intended

risk management A structured approach to eliminating the causes of potential problems *and* planning mitigating actions to minimise the impact of a problem should it happen. The best risk management programmes are committed to paper (or web-tool) and the outputs are integrated into business-as-usual, not stored in a dormant file on somebody's C-Drive

scenario management A simple method for evaluation of options based on constructing and evaluating the likelihood of the working scenario into which the solution will be launched. Scenario management deals in changing the levels of certain variables (e.g. costs, timescales, resource) and the assessment of probability (high–medium–low)

skill development – facilitation One-to-one or group facilitation is often used to transfer a skill and simultaneously to realise a level of value (practical RoI) for the team. A risk with facilitation is that the team takes a back seat and ownership remains with the facilitator

skill development – training Training workshops are a quick, simple and relatively inexpensive tool for transferring new skills into a workforce (e.g. around negotiation or project management). Care must be given to incorporate and sustain learnings to ensure that they do not remain theoretical but can be transferred to realise a practical value

SMT Senior management team – typically managers of strategic functions or business units and responsible for setting (and delivering) strategy

span of control The amount of time given to somebody before they are asked for an update on progress

sponsor A senior manager (or funding customer) who is motivated by the output of a project and who will help clear obstacles to ensure effective execution

stakeholder(s) Any person or group of people who is affected by or who has to live with (use) the outputs of a piece of work

stakeholder management A structured process for ensuring that stakeholder buy-in is maximised – typically through consultation and trying to ensure that their needs are addressed

strategic charter A simple one-page document setting out vision, KPIs, and key enablers/deliverables. Used for reviewing strategic goals, tracking progress and to sell strategy to stakeholders

strategic timeframe The timeframe set for planning strategy. Dictated by the pace of change in the business. Typically 3–5 years

SWOT analysis Analyses strengths, weaknesses, opportunities and threats as basis for understanding the working scenario and developing steps to improve operational or strategic performance

strategy The structure which will serve as a guide for all actions

systems The enabling mechanics which businesses use to automate and drive efficiency of processes and other operational tasks (typically nowadays IT-related)

tactics The on the ground actions which are guided by a strategic framework and which if effectively executed will deliver the corporate goals and vision

team A group of individuals with a common goal that recognises the importance of each individual's contribution in achieving that goal

trust The conviction that a person's actions can and will take your needs into account

value (proposition) The positive impact you will have (or be perceived to have) on the business and your working environment

vision A simply articulated and regularly communicated picture of where you want your part of the business to be in 2–5 years' time

white space The hand-off point or interface between two elements of a process which can often be poorly understood or unclearly mapped – resulting in confusion and delay. (see ownership).

INDEX

Page numbers in **bold** relate to entries in the Glossary

EVERYTHING YOU NEED TO ACCELERATE YOUR CAREER

9780273719922

9780273721765

9780273719908

9780273721802

9780273721789

9780273719885

9780273732907

9780273732884

9780273732860

A complete resource to get ahead as a manager – faster, bringing together the latest business thinking, cutting edge online material and all the practical techniques you need to fast track your career.